An English Countryside Explored

An English Countryside Explored

The Land of Lettice Sweetapple

Peter Fowler & Ian Blackwell

To three generations of
the Swanton family,
of North Farm, West Overton,
who first let us in
and then kept us going

First published in 1998 as *Land of the Lettice Sweetapple*
First published in 2000 as *The English Countryside Explored*

This edition first published in 2009

The History Press
The Mill, Brimscombe Port
Stroud, Gloucestershire, GL5 2QG
www.thehistorypress.co.uk

British Library Cataloguing in Publication Data.
A catalogue record for this book is available from the British Library.

ISBN 978 0 7524 5020 9

Typesetting and origination by The History Press
Printed in Great Britain

CONTENTS

The Illustrations

The *front cover* shows the Valley of Stones, Fyfield

Black and white figures (bold in text)

Colour plates (colour plate bold in text)

Preface

This book is about a small area of countryside in Wiltshire, England. It is also about some of the ways in which that countryside has been explored during the second half of the twentieth century to try to discover what has happened there to give the landscape its present appearance. We believe the resultant story to be typical of many places in southern England. It is not about famous people or well-known events. Rather is it about a local landscape which deals in changes, great and small, and hundreds of thousands of largely anonymous people who lived there and worked the land over 10,000 years. Lettice Sweetapple is one of the relatively few whose name we know. Her life spanned AD 1800. This book's story ends soon after that. Of course, the story itself continues to the present.

The book is based upon a long-term academic study to be formally published as a Research Report of the Society of Antiquaries of London under the title *Landscape Plotted and Pieced. Field archaeology and local history in Fyfield and Overton, Wiltshire*. From that work have come our primary evidence, material and ideas. Here, however, we have had to be very selective, with little room to present original detail or develop our arguments properly. Any qualms on that score are offset, however, by the knowledge that during 1995-8 we rounded off the project professionally. An ordered archive with all the primary and much of the inferential evidence will be in the library and museum of the Wiltshire Archaeological and Natural History Society, Devizes, Wiltshire, with copies on fiche and electronic disc at, and available from, the National Monuments Record, Swindon, Wiltshire. A full electronic archive lodged with the Archaeology Data Service, University of York, is accessible on the Internet at http://ads.ahols.ac.uk/catalogue/. A substantial draft monograph of the Research Report, including three volumes of detailed reports on the excavated material and environmental evidence by the Trust for Wessex Archaeology, is part of that archive. In the nature of things, this short book, which falls into place as a third strand of publication after the archive and the monograph, is likely to be published first. In it, we have felt reasonably free to speculate and use our imagination, seriously and in fun, sometimes going beyond what might well be regarded as legitimate limits in academically correct interpretation.

The project, quietly and periodically jogging on very much part-time from year to year, has been truly amateur in the proper sense until the current professional push needed to bring it to completion. One of us (IWB) became involved at that stage; the other has lived with Fyfield and Overton since 1959. We have come to know our little patch well. We now realise quite a lot about it and suspect that all of England is comparable; more importantly, we now have some grasp of what to ask about it. We wish we could start again, knowing what we now know, for we have hardly begun.

Peter Fowler and Ian Blackwell, University of Newcastle upon Tyne, 30 September 1997

Note: this paperback reprint is not a revised edition of the 1998 hardback, but we have taken the opportunity to adjust the Prologue and the Epilogue to take account of the Sweetapple family genealogy which has been brought to our attention as a result of that publication (with grateful acknowledgements to Shirley Matthews and Gracie Bungey). In particular, Lettice herself was a little older than we inferred. Rather than her death being between 1815-20 as we guessed, at the age of 70 she was buried at Overton on 5 August 1805. The funeral service was presumably in the church as illustrated in our new **colour plate 1**.

Note: In this reprint of the paperback published in 2000 we are able to revise further the life of Lettice Sweetapple as summarised in the Postscript on p. 150 and in some adjustments to the text.

Peter Fowler and Ian Blackwell, January 2009

PROLOGUE:

Lettice Sweetapple in Fact

There was nothing unusual about Lettice Sweetapple except possibly her name.

Lettice lived in a house in West Overton, Wiltshire, just over 200 years ago. It lay alongside the village street opposite the manor farm which had been there since at least medieval times. The village, rather unusually, had probably been founded as a new one a century or so before William the Conqueror became King of England. Lettice has been forgotten and her house is no longer there, replaced by a terrace of farm-labourers' brick cottages in the later nineteenth century. One of them was the Post Office; her house was close by, on its left as you look at it from the front.

The Lord of the Manor was the Earl of Pembroke and Lettice was his tenant. The manor farm would have obstructed Lettice's view from her front windows to the river and the northern downs beyond; but that is not there either. Were she able to look out now on the site where the manor farm had been, she would see a slightly bumpy grass field where horses graze. In her time, she would have looked across at the home of Edward Pumphrey — and the village stocks.

Her neighbour, John Cook, was of an old village family and not so long ago he had leased the manor house. Even now Jane Cook and John the Younger held all the land along the road which led south, out of the village to Hookland. Lettice could see this from her back window, part of a fine view across the manorial open fields, all on the southern downs. She could even see some of her own strips of land in Windmill Field, part of the family inheritance which she held for life — or so she thought until Enclosure (1802) saw them taken from her. Further south, but just out of sight behind her nearer horizon along the top of Windmill Hill, lay the western edge of Savernake Forest. Below her, behind the house, was her garden and in it was a long building. On her west, in the first house you come to in West Overton when arriving along Kennet Drove from the Ridgeway, lived Mrs Martin, a widow. Now in her sixties, she held a large amount of land in West Overton, including Upper and Lower Chichangles woods. Another woman, Elizabeth Seymour, was also a significant landholder.

Lettice's land-holdings were dispersed across the valley slopes and the southern hills. By the River Kennet she had a plot of meadow called North Mead, between the water-mill and the London Road. She also held Long Ground and, further west, Hill Ground, a couple of enclosed and hedged fields either side of Kennet Drove. Her main holding, however, was as strips in the furlongs of the three open fields of West Overton manor. Ditch Hedge Field and Double Hedge Field lay along the western and southern sides of Windmill Field, all three occupying an area already long-cultivated, probably for 3000 years. Some of her strips were grouped together. Over at Savernake Park, at the far south-eastern corner of the estate, she held a square block of 15 acres (6.7ha) up against the hedge which divided West Overton from Lockeridge and Oare Common. Not long since that land had been heath and she was benefiting, with others, from recent clearance and enclosure.

To the west, by the old Huish road, she and some other villagers held strips in what was called Pickrudge Wood, formerly known as *Chichangles Pekethicket*. Pickrudge was wooded in 1734 but in Lettice's time fifty years later, its area was being ploughed. '. . . little Wood in this Lot', remarked the map-maker; but the intake was soon abandoned and Pickrudge Wood reverted to woodland.

The later life of Lettice Sweetapple was bound up with Enclosure. It changed her life, her land, her neighbours and her view. From the later eighteenth century onwards, Edward Pumphrey was acquiring much of West Overton, not least by buying up the tenants' small plots. He no doubt bought all or some of Lettice's holding, perhaps soon after the rent rise of 1802 when the small-holders were in no position to resist a cash offer from an ambitious and successful neighbour who was also an increasingly powerful landlord. Pumphrey prospered and built West Overton Farm in Home Mead just outside the old village, a hundred yards west of Lettice's cottage (**colour plate 32**). It consisted of quite a grand mansion with a model farm behind it. In front was a garden, giving the house fine views north across the regulated flood plain of the Kennet to the London–Bath highway on the other side of the river and the downland pasture beyond. A high red-brick wall screened house and garden from the village and the road linking the village to the highway. Now, no-one overlooked Pumphrey, not even Lettice.

A long history of the land of Lettice Sweetapple precedes these ordinary, typical events. Such village doings some 200 years ago took place on a landscape that was already very, very old. Similar things had been happening for thousands of years. People like Lettice, mixed up with equivalents of the Cooks, Martins, Pumphreys and Pembrokes, had been fashioning these lands for millennia. Sometimes they did so deliberately, as when persons unknown picked Overton Hill as a place for ceremonial buildings about 2000 BC and, 2000 years later, the north side of the River Kennet for the course of their Roman road; just as known individuals did likewise later, for example Edward Pumphrey with his fashionable house and the 1st Earl of Pembroke who created an early seventeenth-century hunting park which has left its imprint on the landscape of the twentieth century. Most of the time, however, most peoples' concerns were domestic, agricultural, religious, personal, with little if any thought for the effects of their actions.

Exactly the same is true for all those centuries back from 1800, back through the Middle Ages to 1066 and beyond that through Saxon and Roman times to the anonymity of prehistory. Little cameos like that of Lettice, outlined here from primary archaeological, documentary and cartographic evidence, could be repeated in Fyfield and Overton countless times back to 10,000 years ago. Essentially the people throughout were like us and, even more importantly, we are like they were.

This should help us to understand what was going on. To cultivate such understanding, we just have to be reasonable, observant and patient. Our heroine might well have come up with such a commonplace, and why not?

There is nothing unusual about Lettice Sweetapple except possibly her name, and even that is readily explicable. Although 'Lettice' is of course the diminuitive of 'Laetaetia', 'Lettice' as such was used at least twice in the Sweetapple family, a family documented from the seventeenth century and becoming well-established in Hampshire and north Wiltshire in the eighteenth and nineteenth centuries.

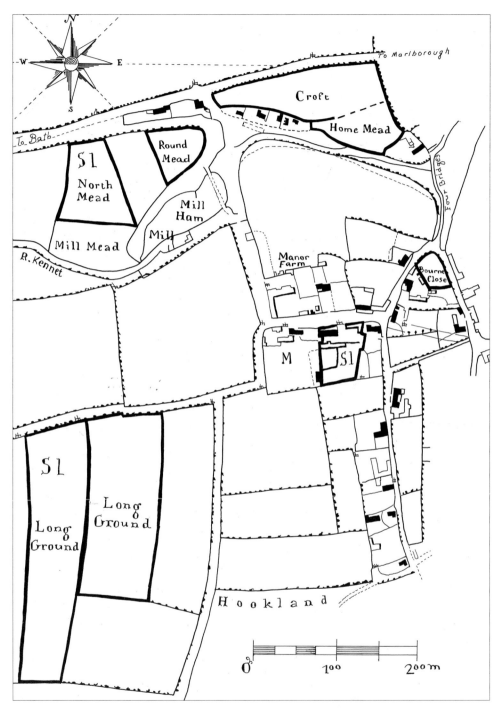

1 *Map of West Overton village in 1794, copied from the manorial map, showing lands held by Lettice Sweetapple (Sl and outlined in heavy black). For comparison, the lands held by another lady of the village, Elizabeth Seymour, are also outlined heavily (but not lettered). The village seems to have consisted of only 16 houses (solid black) at the time. Lettice's was a substantial property with outbuildings directly opposite the manor house and flanked by Mrs Martin's property (M) on the west.*

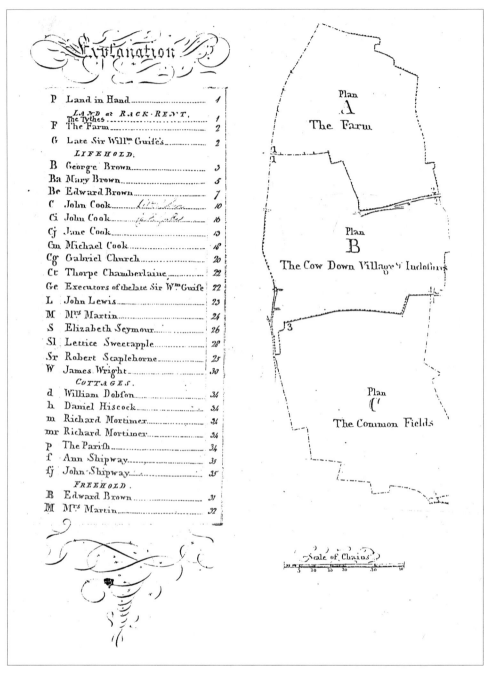

2 *Lifeholders in West Overton Manor, 1794, including Lettice Sweetapple. Her name, with her abbreviation 'Sl'*
('Sweetapple, Lettice') is among the lifeholders, between Elizabeth Seymour and Robert Scaplehorne. The list is
the key, or 'Explanation', to four maps which delineate the Manor in some detail. We use the fourth one (D) as
*the basis for **71**; the areas the other three (A-C) cover are shown here on what is a reduced copy of the original top*
page of the document. The map itself does not have a written date on it so our '1794', though well-founded, we
believe, is inferential; the Enclosure map of 1802 is based on this one. Much of our information about the period
and Lettice herself comes from this map.

PART I: A PLACE

1

A sense of place

Fyfield and Overton could be anywhere in southern England. Pleasant-looking villages, they snuggle into their countryside in a way taken as so very English. Both are clearly 'old', for at the very least they have old-looking churches. A visitor, having heard of neither Fyfield nor Overton, could easily wonder, nevertheless, whether they were in any proper sense 'historic'. Nobody famous has ever emerged from the ordinariness of either of these places, yet these villages and their countryside as they exist now are the product of a long and extremely complex process. In fact they are deeply historic, if history is about the ordinary and typical as well as the famous and the flashy.

The two villages are in Wiltshire between London and Bath. Locally, they are south of Swindon and between Marlborough and Calne, just a couple of miles south-east of Avebury. They lie in the gentle valley of the River Kennet, on the south side of the new (1743) London to Bath road, now the A4. This location is important for two reasons. We must be certain, in the first place, which Fyfield and Overton we are talking about, for both these place-names are common. There is another Fyfield in south Wiltshire, for example, and another way to the north-east near Oxford. At least ten Overtons exist. One is near Andover in Hampshire. Indeed one of our first questions might well be to ask why these two villages have such common names. Overton tells us that the early settlement was described as an 'upper farm' (from the Old English *ufera tun*), situated up from the floodplain of the river (not high up on the downs). Fyfield means 'five hides', the normal holding of a thegn in tenth-century England. So one place-name refers to a common location for a farm, the other to a common tenurial arrangement in late Saxon times. So, yes, our villages are undistinguished, yet the very commonness of their names hints at some basic truth about the English countryside.

One problem in keeping our inquiry under control is that, straight away, such simple questions immediately prompt others. Where was this 'upper farm' ? Who was the thegn? Why are there just two villages when there might well have been, say, eight? In fact there have been eight, and that is just for medieval times onwards! What do we mean by 'English'? Whatever we mean, had we better not be careful in just assuming that both our apparently common-o' garden villages are 'English'? Originally, we discovered, one of them was not.

The other main reason for being quite clear about where we are is that the land of our enquiry has its own particular character. In one sense we could be anywhere in southern England (or at least in the Chalk country), but in another sense the land of Lettice Sweetapple is a very distinctive place. In that sense, we could not be anywhere else. Why is that so? In what ways is that land distinctive? What are its characteristics? How can we recognise, describe and explain them?

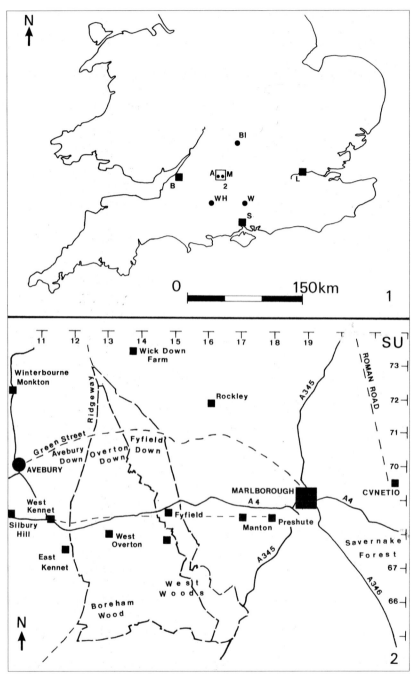

3 Location of the Land of Lettice Sweetapple: 1 (top) in central southern England in the box between Bristol (B) and London (L) and, locally, Avebury (A) and Marlborough (M). S is Southampton. The other three places (circles) are those with which the parishes of Fyfield and West Overton were particularly associated: Bl Blenheim WH Wilton W Winchester; 2 is the boxed area above at a larger scale with the 1 km intervals of the National Grid indicated to the top and the right, showing the two parishes (heavy broken lines), four pre-modern (thin dashed lines) and four modern (A4 etc) roads, and some places and names used in the book.

We set out to answer such questions, and soon found that trying to answer proved to be not an act but a process; a process which was quite as difficult to be a part of as it was attempting to produce an answer. In any case, we also found that, in a sense, there are no answers and certainly rarely simple ones; the evidence is nearly always absent, fragmentary or ambiguous. Interpretation comes to be quite as important as research, piling up its little heap of facts. Different questions lead to different evidence; basically what you ask is the sort of history that you get. There is no 'given' history just waiting there for the local historian to reveal, any more than there is a particular truth under the ground awaiting its discovery by its chosen archaeologist. There is no one history of Fyfield and Overton. Different facts suggest different interpretations and the same evidence inspires different people to come up with different interpretations; the same person can favour different meanings from the same evidence at different times. Judgement is all, spiced every now and then, as we have enjoyed doing here, with a little flight of fancy. Bluntly, it is sometimes a guess, as we try to knead the rather unwieldy dough of data, interpretation and imagination into some sort of plausible sense, even some sort of story.

Our story is first and foremost about a piece of land rather than the people in it; though we know that it is the two together who have made it the place as it is. Our hero is the land of Lettice Sweetapple, not the woman herself. We sense, however, that the real heroes and heroines are the tens of thousands of largely anonymous people who, over the last 10,000 years or so, have lived in, worked on and been buried under the land we have named after her. She herself was, like 99.9% of those people, not particularly important or distinguished. Lettice is rescued only from the anonymity of most of her fellow inhabitants by the fact that she was a 'lifeholder' in the manor of West Overton, holding land for life as a tenant and notably in its great common fields as shown on maps of 1794 and, at Enclosure, in 1802. Her holdings, and her name, appear, as do those of other land holders of various standing, like Edward Brown and Gabriel Church.

These were the sort of people, and the very individuals, who stood to lose most as the land was formally enclosed hereabouts by Acts of Parliament over the following twenty-five years. The creation of the 1794 map was the first step towards this process; it was used as the basis for the 1802 map which was not, we suspect, newly resurveyed. Yet, while individuals' circumstances were indeed changed as the big landowners, here the Earl of Pembroke and the Duke of Marlborough, consolidated their holdings, in some respects the landscape itself was only partly modified rather than radically changed. The common fields where Lettice had held her strips, for example, did indeed change in their tenure and mode of working, but visually the area they occupied remained open. The land was not divided up by lots of new hedges, as in other parts of England, and most of Windmill Hill continues to this day as a rather windy expanse of arable field.

Similarly, north of the Kennet, West Overton's old pasture was not hedged either and still remains as an extensive open area of valley slope, though long since cultivated (**70, colour plate 2**). It would be very easy today for, say, an eagle-eyed but superficially-informed countryside campaigner or planning officer to think they were looking at dreary landscapes created for prairie-farming by mid-twentieth-century hedge removal; but the historical fact is that hedges have never enclosed these open spaces. What we are looking at are expanses, without the strip fields, of what much of this West Overton downland countryside looked like throughout medieval times — treeless, hedgeless, windy, cold and, on wet and cloudy days, drear; so let us not confuse prettiness with historicity.

4 Fyfield Down, 1960: the essence of downland archaeology as it then was, grass and sarsen stones which are still there, but with a shepherd's hut on wheels, a shepherded flock, youth and imperial ranging poles, all of which have disappeared into the mist of time like that prevailing when this photograph was taken.

Further north, on what continued to be great sheep pastures, very little actual enclosure occurred either (**4**); just specific pieces like Parson's Penning on Hackpen Down were hedged or fenced. And though lines were officiously drawn on maps over much of this down, nothing actually happened on the ground. Clearly the great landscape change brought about by Enclosure elsewhere was, in our two parishes, very much a bits and pieces affair, drastically affecting tenure and agricultural practice but not immediately or radically changing the appearance of the land of Lettice Sweetapple as a whole.

So the story we try to tell is not just about the people nor merely of the villages. We look at the whole area contained within the two parishes of present-day Fyfield and West Overton, an area of about 7000 acres (2834ha). This story lies in their fields, on their downs, in their woods: that is where run the books we read. We get out and about into the surrounding countryside, the landscape where Derby-winning racehorses are (sometimes) trained; where a brewing family's estate in the nineteenth century very much affected what we see today; where Lettice held her 25 strips before Enclosure; where the Pembroke estate benefited enormously from the Dissolution; where thousands of manorial, downland sheep helped support an appropriate monastic life-style at Winchester throughout medieval times; where, in the twelfth century, Knights Templar tried to exploit a new estate put together to support their small community high on the downs and argued with their neighbours; where ancient estates are actually described in Domesday Book and land charters either side of AD 950; where hundreds, if not thousands, laboured to construct Wansdyke about AD 500 and where, 400 years earlier, a Roman countryside equipped with main road, lanes, villages and blocks of rectilinear fields appeared. A landscape of prehistory, where extensive farmed areas dominated an organised downland in the second millennium BC; and where, by 2000 BC, the downs themselves had been created from post-glacial forest by hunters and then, in the biggest change ever to occur hereabouts, the arrival of farmers. Farming, perhaps remarkably after its first appearance here some 5000-6000 years ago, still dominates this landscape. The landscape continues to change.

A theory lies behind all this, of course. It is a theory neatly encapsulated nowadays in the phrase 'landscape archaeology', though most of the methods and thinking involved have for long been practised by archaeologists, especially field archaeologists, geologists, especially geomorphologists, historians, especially local historians, and geographers, especially historical geographers. The network is even wider, for some of the principles and some of the methods of natural historians, such as field botanists or foresters, are commonly shared. Landscape archaeology embraces the approaches and many of the methods of all these, and others, in as far as they help elucidate the long-term history of landscape. Usually this means a particular landscape, though its scale can vary from continent to a field. The theory is that it is worthwhile to try to understand such a landscape by establishing what it was like at the beginning, in Britain usually meaning as it emerged from the last Ice Age about 12,000 years ago. The idea is then to define changes, the processes by which they occurred and, if possible, the reasons for changes occurring and the consequences of such changes up to the present day.

5 Surveying on Overton Down: instrumental surveying, here with a plane table, was a basic technique used in recording and interpreting sites. This particular one, superficially a jumble of slight earthworks even in the relief afforded by a low winter sun, seemed to be a Romano-British settlement with a post-Roman enclosure beside it which we suggest might be one of the missing Saxon sheep-cotes. Collin Bowen is indicating that its bank, on which he is standing, continues to the east; Inigo Jones is marking the line of the Saxon 'Overton Ridgeway' — and keeping an eye on the cattle for whom surveying equipment possesses an irresistible attraction. The trees on the skyline are on Martinsell Hill, above Oare, one of the highest points in the area.

6 Raddun, Fyfield Down: detecting features underground in November 1962, using an early miniaturised resistivity meter in the hands of its scientific developer, the late Tony Clark.

The basic premise is that the bulk of the evidence, especially the key evidence, is out there in the field, on and under the ground surface (**5**). Close behind this comes an often unstated secondary belief that we have between us a suite of tried and tested principles, like stratigraphy and sampling theory, backed up by a battery of proven field methodologies and practices, themselves nowadays increasingly implemented by a range of instrumentation, e.g. 'total stations' for surveying out of doors and scanning microscopes for laboratory analysis. In our case, we used geophysics a lot in the early days, especially resistivity and magnetometer sub-terrestial surveying. Then it was fairly bow-wave technique; now the equipment looks antediluvian. Most recently we have learnt as much about prehistoric botany from soil analysis in the laboratory as we have about late Saxon flora from our tenth-century land charters (**6-9, colour plate 3-4**).

In the all-embracing approach of the landscape archaeologist, the type of evidence to hand is, in a sense, no more important than the technique used to examine it; and that applies just as much to oral, documentary and cartographic evidence which, again in much-used landscapes such as those of Britain, is quite as likely to be available and pertinent as old buildings and pollen grains from a buried soil. The crucial thing is what every bit of relevant evidence can tell you about your landscape. Then the challenge comes: putting it all together, melding it, and judging what it 'means'. The project behind the exploration of the historic landscape of Fyfield and Overton which we write about here was based on this sort of thinking and those sorts of methods.

Though we have studied only a tiny patch of England's surface, we have added to the area's general interest by looking at the whole of two parishes, not just one, thereby being able to explore some unexpected dynamics. Our understanding was further helped when we decided early on to break away from the downs, with their obvious archaeology, to look at the whole of the two parishes south of the river Kennet (**colour plate 5**). This not only increased the size of our picture-frame, but gave us a much more sensible area to work with; for, allowing for minor modern changes, the parishes consist of anciently defined, real, live working landscapes, not just arbitrary chunks defined by academics. This approach also added a significant dimension to our thinking; the parishes lie in parallel strips across the river valley, stretching southwards from those northern downs across a variety of terrain and natural resources to, of all things in chalk country, heath (**11**).

In practice, however, we could not examine the whole area at the same standard of intensity, so our work was split into three levels and three zones. It is interesting to us now that this purely logistical, methodological factor has very much affected our sense of this place. The core area, which included all the excavations, was a small one on the downs. Around it was a zone where we examined the whole of the land surface systematically and carried out metrical survey on the ground. In an outer, peripheral zone we carried out reconnaissance fieldwork. If only we had another decade to work out the history of this area in as much detail as the downs. Nevertheless, this largely self-selecting methodology, and the much wider area which was embraced, raised yet more related and subsidiary questions, but the basic one remained 'How did this landscape come to look like this?'. The difference was, as Chapters 7-10 explore, that we were now looking to explain much more than a downland landscape.

7 Raddun, Fyfield Down: explaining what was happening and why excavation of a medieval long-house would be done in a particular (as it happened, wrong) way to volunteer excavators on Whit Saturday, 16 May 1959.

We talk of a small place but of a long time, at least in the human perspective. We find people baffled by one of the crucial characteristics of this place. 'Why is it', they ask, 'that all this very old stuff, your prehistoric sites you claim to have found, why are they on the ground or even sticking up out of it? Why are they not buried deep below the grass (**colour plate 4**)?' In

*8 Raddun, Fyfield Down: photographing a medieval long-house (**43**). Photography is an essential part of the record, and height is often necessary to obtain an appropriate view of the subject. This photograph, from the early days of the project, illustrates the principle, though the method is not recommended — and in any case, it would nowadays contravene safety requirements. The platform on an hydraulic hoist, as used for inspecting overhead cables or by firemen, is ideal for the purpose.*

particular when we were excavating on Overton Down, visitors were frankly incredulous that a settlement nearly 3000, and burials nearly 4000 years old, were at the same level, only about 10in (25cm) below where they stood. The answer lies in changes through time, in processes like erosion and land-use. We turn to such matters in our local landscape in the next chapter.

9 Delling Copse, Fyfield: pottery and other material is here being given initial treatment in the field as it comes off the excavation — washing, marking, sorting, bagging and boxing. Nowadays better conditions and more standardised materials would be normal, but the principles remain the same. The desirability of acquiring working space under cover close to the excavation has led to many different sorts of premises being pressed into temporary archaeological service: here the redundant game-bird sheds and pig-sties attached to a gamekeeper's cottage provided a useful base.

2

Local landscape

The Sweetapple countryside lies on chalk, technically not in just one solid lump but in three layers, Upper (the latest), Middle and Lower (the earliest and hardest). The nature of the top six feet (2m) so of this Upper Chalk was well illustrated when an experimental earthwork was built on it in 1960 on Overton Down (**colour plate 7**). Just how effectively nature will re-clothe supposedly 'bare' chalk, given certain circumstances, has been demonstrated within a generation (**10**). Our own area excavations nearby exposed the fragility of this Chalk's crumbly surface only nine inches or so (23cm) below the down land turf (**35, colour plate 17**).

Such a Chalk geology gives this countryside several characteristics. It is a relatively young landscape in geological terms, for chalk is one of the last of the natural rocks to have been laid down, as sediment at the bottom of a sea covering what is now southern England some 65 million years ago. This should not be taken to imply that the earliest Fyfieldians were fish. Nevertheless, such creatures swam in what is now the sky above where Lettice was much later to live, and their fossils survive in the fields and gardens of the area.

The fact that chalk underlies this whole landscape provides us with one of the basic clues as to what human life here was going to be like. Because the bedrock was chalk, then it was likely, for example, that people living here would tend to have a water problem — lots of it could erode the soft bedrock and the light soils that tend to develop on chalk; too little of it could quickly create a water shortage because of the chalk's immense, sponge-like capacity to soak up surface water and store it at considerable depth in great underground reservoirs. As historians

10 *Experimental earthwork, Overton Down 1993, cf.* **colour plate 7** *showing it 33 years earlier.*

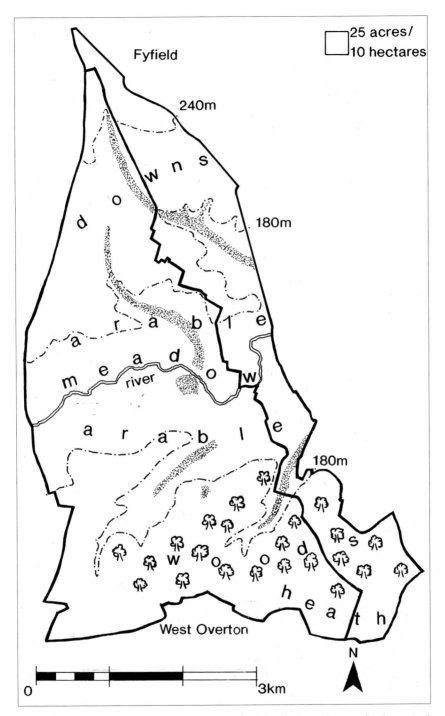

11 Map: Fyfield and West Overton parishes: basic resources and land-use. The area of study contained considerable trains of sarsen stones (stippled) as well as the other natural resources of river and woods. The river has been exploited for millennia. The woods persist to the south, but have given way elsewhere to heath and, most notably, downland. The broad land-use zones of pasture on the downs, arable, meadow and woodland management represent a human imposition on a heavily modified landscape.

23

we could confidently expect to find evidence, on the one hand, of use and careful husbanding of water supplies and, on the other, disputes about who owned which water.

This softish chalk is what gives our area of countryside its shape. The River Kennet begins at the foot of the chalk escarpment a few miles to the north-west: it should perhaps have gone west and flowed into the Bristol Avon, the Severn Estuary and the Atlantic Ocean. Instead, it turned left, finding a weak enough fault in the chalk to break through it and create its own valley as it flowed eastwards into the Thames and the North Sea. So our little area is at a hinge point in the countryside; it is one of those proverbial places where two raindrops, one on either side of a line, can end up in two different oceans. The raindrop that went east trickled slowly across and through the chalk towards what, aeons later, were to become Reading and London, and thus began to set the course of what eventually became the valley of the River Kennet draining into the River Thames.

The headwaters of the Kennet are disputed, some arguing they lie up the stream beyond Avebury and others correctly seeing them as a spring on the side of a low bluff on which Silbury Hill was to be built much later. These two streams have been distinguished by two names, the Avebury Winterbourne and a name lost during the last thousand years, the Og, apparently a local name for the stretch between Silbury and Overton. They became the infant River Kennet which was strong enough to cut the west-facing escarpment of the Marlborough Downs. The valley sides, even now, are nowhere steep or dramatic; the slope south from Overton Hill and just east of Fyfield church at the two edges of the parishes are as great as any (**colour plate 6**).

So the valley generally came to have long, gentle sides. Its south-facing northern side is particularly attractive to farmers but the north-facing southern slopes seem to have been used just as much over the centuries. Flowing along on or only slightly into the harder Lower Chalk, the river came to follow numerous sinuous courses along the valley floor. In some places, as at Lockeridge, it deposited gravel, a material quarried in medieval times. Elsewhere, the vagaries of the water-flow had the effect of cutting locally-prominent little bluffs, where the Middle or Lower Chalk resisted erosion. Overton church stands on one, Fyfield church on another. This valley, so typical of English chalkland in many respects, is then natural, yet it is also the product of centuries of human activity (**12**).

The villages and farms are not in fact on the river bank, for the valley here has a slight but well-marked flood plain. Just above the flood plain is a minor shelf and it is here that people first dwelt, or at least they appear to have done so since Roman times. Before then, the flood plain was a surface that was in general continually rising. Worked flints and other evidence of habitation from about 8000 years ago are buried some 6ft (2m) below the present ground level, evidence enough that water-borne silts and rain-washed soil from the valley sides were being deposited into the valley, probably over thousands of years. Allowance also has to be made for 'events' as well as long-term process. A flash-flood, for example, could make big changes in a short time. Some material undoubtedly flowed in from the side-valleys, from what are now the dry-valleys like Pickledean. Good evidence of 'soil-creep' has come from there, perhaps from about 3000 years ago.

Since the Roman period, however, the ground level of the valley floor has hardly risen. Its surface is pock-marked and crinkled with the signs of people trying in various ways over the last 2000 years to make safe crossings, improve the water-flow, control the river course, employ the water-power and make their valley-bottom fields more fertile. There were, for example, mills here, though none now exists, and water-meadows, constructed under Act of Parliament in 1821, replaced earlier ones in a tradition which may well go back to Anglo-Saxon times.

12 *Looking west in winter towards the burial mounds silhouetted on Overton, or Seven Barrow, Hill from beside the footbridge over the River Kennet at the end of Frog Lane where the Saxon boundary between West and East Overton still runs.*

The movement of water and the growth of the River Kennet have also given the valley a key position in terms of human movement. As a result of its formation, people can move eastwards by an overland route, from the Bath and Bristol area, past Fyfield and Overton, down the Kennet valley and into the Thames basin. This opening also has the big advantage of being a direct route. Otherwise, travellers from the west would have had no choice but to trek northwards round the Marlborough Downs and then past Swindon into the Thames valley or south eastwards through the difficult Vale of Pewsey or round the south of Salisbury Plain itself. The Kennet valley is, then, a key west-east communication corridor, formalised by the building of the London to Bath Roman road through it (3). Surprisingly, however, this route was ignored by the railway which went precisely along the three other routes just outlined. It gave, and still gives, access to different resources, creating new lines of communication and, ultimately, leading through London to Europe. But, as the Roman road implies, a way out can also be a way in.

Movement along the Kennet valley and across the subtle watershed on Overton Hill both eastwards and to the west was predictable and became an obvious feature of the history of the area. What was not so clear was that our parishes were in fact to become a sort of countryside cross-roads on the grand scale. Traffic from north and south also crossed this landscape, fording and later bridging the Kennet rather than going along its valley. Echoed nowadays in the name and minor function of the Ridgeway along our western bounds, this north/south–south/north movement is an aspect of this landscape that has almost been forgotten. Historically it was, however, once important, and our recognition of this is one of our major 'discoveries' about the area.

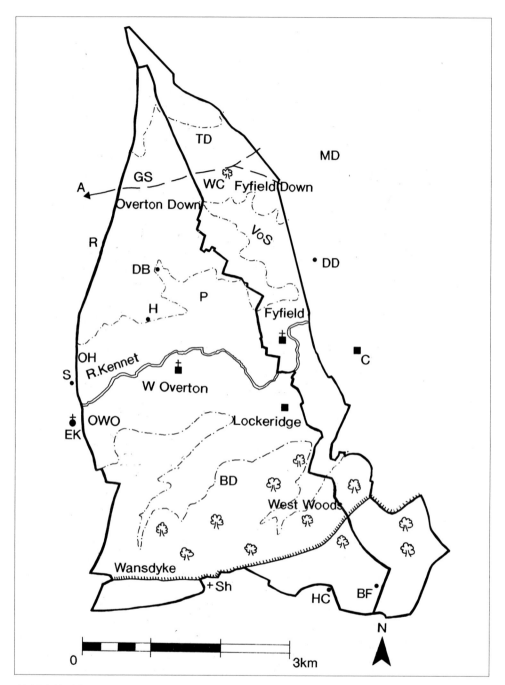

13 *Fyfield and West Overton Civil Parishes: some names in the landscape which are either or both significant and used often in this book.*

Key: *A Avebury BD Boreham Down BF Bayardo Farm C Clatford DB Down Barn DD Devil's Den EK East Kennet GS Green Street H Headlands HC Heath Cottage MD Manton Down OH Overton Hill OWO old West Overton P Pickledean R The Ridgeway S the Sanctuary Sh Shaw TD Totterdown VoS Valley of Stones WC Wroughton Copse*

The shape of the land, its topography, was one of the factors creating the circumstances for this ancient north-south route. Basically, the chalk deposit, now the Marlborough Downs, has been worn and cut down across its upper surfaces by ice, wind, rain, frost and the effects of temperature change over hundreds of thousands of years. One result is that now the highest chalk faces north, looking out over the Upper Thames valley. From there, marked on Barbury Down by a late prehistoric hillfort, the land slopes generally southwards, dissected by numerous, now dry, valleys or combes trending north-west down to the south-east. This has created a landscape inviting travel along the ridge-tops. The ground is usually dry, locally you are not overlooked and you have a sense of being on top of the world provided by the distant views beneath big skies — these afford easy passage, safety and pleasure to the walker and horse-rider.

So the landscape of Fyfield and Overton is laced with paths and tracks coming down off the Downs into the valley, crossing the river, then easing their way up the north-facing slopes of the Kennet valley and thence down into the Vale of Pewsey. One destination was market — one of the great sheep markets of medieval England such as Salisbury or Yarnbury — but beyond was another, the Channel ports and Europe, which certainly exercised a pull far inland from well before the Romans. So landscape and traffic, land-form and travelling, interact in this local landscape, the one encouraging the other, the other influencing the shape of the human countryside as it developed over the centuries on top of the natural landscape.

The rolling downland so characteristic of this area now is natural in its shape but not in its superficial appearance. Its openness has been created and its now relatively rare grass-cropped surface is as artificial as the ploughland which has commonly replaced it. Again, we explore the basis of such generalisations later. Here we note that Lettice's landscape, as she herself must have often been grateful for, contains much more than open downland. In particular, the southern quarter of the two parishes of Fyfield and Overton is thickly wooded, which is unusual for most chalkland parishes. This is an aspect of the Fyfield and Overton countryside also borne out by documents, of which more later. It is the fact of the woodland, now as previously, which is another key to understanding this bit of England. It gives us some idea of how extensive forest cover may once have been and what parts of it may have looked like, not as unkempt wild wood but as a managed resource. Ten thousand years ago post-glacial wild wood probably covered all our area. West Woods, as this wood is known, certainly an area of woodland since prehistoric times, is a relic of that ancient forest, though its present well-managed appearance and its make-up partly of non-indigenous soft-woods betray the effects of twentieth-century silviculture. Nevertheless, we know that it has been managed since medieval times and can infer the same was true earlier (**14, colour plate 5**).

Though chalk lies under the woods, the trees themselves are growing in an overlying layer of clay-with-flints. Such land is obviously more difficult to work than the light, crumbly soils on the chalk itself, but it holds water longer and its nutrients tend not to be washed away by rain. Indeed, it is not as subject to erosion as are the chalk soils. Nevertheless, land on clay-with-flints tends to be used as a secondary resource, at least from the point of view of the arable farmer, so patches of it are often left as rough grazing, scrub or woodland. It extends over much of the high downland to the north and, though no permanent woodland exists there as in West Woods, Wroughton Copse is on it and likely to be a patch of medieval woodland which colonised Roman fields. Higher up, Totterdown Wood, though a plantation, highlights an area of rough grazing where once Roman fields were also ploughed and where gorse now flowers (**colour plate 4**).

*14 Wools (or Wolfs) Grove in West Woods, showing a typical young plantation renewing the timber stock as has been practised here for millennia. The bank on the right, part of a former woodland enclosure, is one of the highest earthworks in the Woods apart from a long barrow (**colour plate 26**) and Wansdyke (**colour plate 5**) but is otherwise characteristic of the medieval or later field archaeology of these Woods.*

If chalk and clay-with-flints are typical of the Wiltshire Downs, the outstanding distinctive feature of Lettice's countryside is the sarsen stone. This exists as blocks of sandstone, the remains of a former seabed which broke up and scattered bits and pieces across an emerging landscape. In and just after the last glaciation, the 'as-yet-to-be' Fyfield and Overton lay in a rather messy, disrupted zone just beyond the glaciers themselves. In such natural conditions, with ice and sludge often thawing and freezing again, season to season and perhaps even day to day, the sarsens tended to move down slope with the surface debris of the glacial fringes. Like the sludge which ended on the lower valley slopes and in the combe bottoms, they assembled in long trains along or just under the new surfaces of the valleys. You can still go and see this phenomenon, notably by the roadside in Lockeridge Dene, courtesy of the National Trust, and, if you are prepared to walk a mile or two keeping to the rights of way, in the Valley of Stones on Fyfield Down (**15, colour plate 8**).

Such sarsen trains today are, however, mere remnants of what once was. Sarsens used to be much more extensive and much denser in their occurrence at favoured places. They have largely been cleared from such, however, since they were first used for building long barrows 6000 years ago. A second small area of sarsens preserved by the National Trust, for example, lies close to but invisible from the A4. This is but a fragment of a former sarsen train in Pickledean stretching up to Down Barn and beyond. You only have to look at the gate-posts, boundary stones and semi-ruinous cattle-yards along this dene to see where lots of the stones have been used just locally, never mind about taken elsewhere. You can, however, see a more extensive array of them spread

15 Sarsen stones on Totterdown, a particularly stony area of high downland on Clay-with-Flints between Overton and Fyfield Downs. Here the view is to the south-east along an early trackway, defined by a lynchet and stone to the left and the scarp on which the figure (Gillian Swanton) is standing on the right. Beyond is the treeless expanse of Fyfield Down dropping down towards Clatford Bottom, with the land rising again across the Kennet valley up to West Woods in the distance.

across Overton Down to the north, but only a relatively small area there is natural. The rest of the visible stones have largely been shifted along the edges of prehistoric and Roman fields. The same is true on the slopes of Totterdown where the sarsens are much thicker on the ground. Even in the Valley of Stones, it is only along the northern reaches of the dry valley that the sarsens lie in profusion. The rest of that Valley has been emptied of stones, mainly during a phase of systematic quarrying that came to an end only in 1939. Though they are not so readily visible because of the woodland, some of the best stretches of partly uncleared sarsens lie in West Woods at the southern end of the parishes, especially along the combes.

The reason for the present fragmentary survival of the sarsen cover is, of course, that stone is all too useful for building. This is especially so in an area where building material other than wood and straw is difficult to come by. Just look at the churches and older houses in the villages and you can see where some of the sarsen has gone. And they are just the tip of the proverbial iceberg: think of all the pre-medieval buildings using sarsen which we can no longer see; think too of the historical records of sarsen having being exported to surface the roads of Swindon New Town and provide kerbstones for the precinct of St Paul's, London (**colour plate 9**).

But another, less obvious reason for their disappearance may in fact have been more important over the millennia. This is a farming area, and has been for 6000 years. Stones get in the way of farming, especially arable farming. Many, many thousands of them have been broken up where possible, or dragged to field edges and sometimes buried. Farming cleared the land of sarsens almost as dramatically as of trees. Buried beneath one field bank on Fyfield Down, for example, was a Roman field wall which included a broken sarsen handmill of prehistoric type. Buried in a great pit in West Overton's South Field, where Lettice held her land, was such a huge dump of sarsen that the Reverend Smith, one of the many Victorian antiquaries to inspect the area, was moved to remark in 1885:

> when …a buried sarsen comes inconveniently near the surface, to the serious discomforture of the carter, whose plough, …horses and harness, as well as himself, receive from it a very rough shock, it is the custom of the agriculturalists to set the stone-cutters to work, to break up and remove such an intruding sarsen. Such a case occurred on Lurkeley Hill; when the stone-cutters …discovered that the sarsen they were about to demolish, …rested on huge blocks of stone. It occupied the stone-cutters many days to break up and remove the large superincumbent sarsen, and then they had to demolish and get out another huge stone ….

This is very much a landscape of and about sarsens. A soldier wrote in his diary in the seventeenth century that men used to be able to walk from Avebury to Marlborough across Overton and Fyfield Downs without touching the ground. The sarsens must have lain in such profusion that a man could leap from one to another all the way - as is still the case in parts of the Valley of Stones. Sarsens are also supposed to 'grow', that is they emerge from the ground where none were previously visible. This is certainly true, and we are only half-convinced by the rational explanation that, when a sarsen lies just under the grass, sun and wind so dry out its thin covering that its surface comes to be exposed. Anyway, they multiply naturally while men taketh them away.

Another oddity is their very name. Sarsen is supposed to be a corruption of *Saracen*. The local folklore has it that the Knights Templar, who held property in this area from the twelfth century to their suppression, returning to base here for recuperation or to retire after fighting real Saracens abroad, found their homeland littered with these foreign looking and oddly hostile stones. Indeed, look carefully and you will notice many of the stones have holes in them. Scientifically, these have been made by roots but mainly by slightly acidic rainwater eating into weak points in the stones' surface. More romantically, some say these were created by the roots of seaweed when the stone was soft and formed the seabed. Others say that they were made by the knights who, after spearing stones which served as *saracens* in the games that Templars played, stuck wooden poles in the hollows on which the heads of the infidels were displayed.

Many locally call the stones *grey wethers*, which normally refers to a castrated male sheep. This arose because it is difficult to distinguish at a distance a clutch of stones from a flock of sheep on a misty day on the downland. And it is no good expostulating 'How ridiculous! Of course you can tell — sheep move for one thing!'. Well, you look hard and long enough through the rain or across the deepening twilight murk at what you think are stones. We leave it to your conscience whether you can swear that not one of them moved (4).

PART II: AN INVESTIGATION

3

Search among the sarsens

One of us (PJF) first went up to Fyfield Down on 7 April 1959. Although he did not know it at the time, it was to be a day not without significance in his life:

'I felt as if I was walking on holy ground, an acolyte being conducted into the temple by the Master. I was young and inexperienced, barely three months into my first archaeological post, yet I knew enough to be in awe of this place; the place, so I had read, where the stones for Stonehenge had come from. I was certainly in awe of my leader who seemed to know everything. I was being led by one of the great field archaeologists of his, or any other, generation, Collin Bowen. The name will probably mean little to the reader but that does not matter. We all have our heroes and Collin, then just my boss, was later to become one.

'We were there for a specific reason. We were looking for two small, circular enclosures made of low banks, linked to form a figure-of-eight. These two enclosures lay on top of longer, earlier banks. Our only evidence for the existence of these banks was a single oblique air photograph taken some time previously by Dr. J.K. St. Joseph of Cambridge University, a pioneer of air photography. Collin Bowen was then writing his short book, 'Ancient Fields', and was therefore particularly interested in the possibility shown by the air photograph that the banks over which the two enclosures had been built might be the edges of an 'ancient field'. If we could date the enclosure, he reasoned, then at least we would have a date by which this particular field, believed to be of a prehistoric type, had gone out of use. I agreed, standing there, somewhere south of Wroughton Copse, in what seemed the middle of nowhere among slightly forbidding stones. It was not just an unfamiliar landscape; it seemed somewhat alien. Yet I was supposed to be starting an excavation here in a month's time ... if we could find the right place.

'In fact Collin walked straight to it, even though it was a 'new' site — that is, it was not on Ordnance Survey maps and had not previously been noted. Or so we thought at the time. Later we discovered that two other people had known about it, even investigated it: one 140 years earlier, the other just a few months before us. Nevertheless, on that day I had my first real lesson in archaeological field recording and interpretation, an innocently seminal occasion since I have been doing that ever since, on Fyfield Down and elsewhere. Our reconnaissance established that the enclosure did indeed overlie ancient fields, or 'Celtic' fields as they were generally called then. Indeed, we thought the enclosures might well contain structures. The chances of dating the site therefore seemed quite good. The search for information and a story was on. Collin and I surveyed the site on 25 April, noting that the enclosures were certainly on top of 'Celtic' field lynchets but that a possible house seemed to be long and rectangular in plan. We did not know of such in prehistoric Wessex. Excavation began over the weekend 9-10 May. The original surveyed site-plan, and the written and photographic records of those days are in the archive, so you can see them should you want to. Several of the photographs are used here (**43, 45**).

'Behind that incident in early Spring on Fyfield Down lay a long history of archaeological fieldwork on the southern English chalkland. During this early work many sites had been found, types recognised, a methodology developed and scholarly understanding committed to paper. By 1959, I was therefore heir to a considerable academic tradition, one I was very conscious of and only too happy to absorb.'

Fyfield Down was part of that heritage, for it was already famous archaeologically, first as the possible source of the Stonehenge stones, as already mentioned, second because of its 'Celtic' fields (**colour plate 10**). They had become well-known because of a particular air photograph which had been used in several books; but the fields themselves had not been studied on the ground. This type of field had been discovered forty years earlier by O.G.S. Crawford, a pioneer field archaeologist and air photographer. The academic need in the late 1950s, as indeed is still the case, was to acquire dates for this type of field. It was known from aerial photographs to spread over considerable areas of the downs in a chequered pattern of small, interlocking squarish enclosures. Crawford applied the adjective *Celtic* to them to place the type squarely in prehistory. He did this to emphasise that these fields were earlier than the familiar medieval open fields and earlier than the long strips of the open fields (then thought to be Anglo-Saxon in origin).

In the 1950s, 'Celtic' fields were believed to be generally of Iron Age date (then 500 BC to AD 43), and yet they had recently been shown by the Ordnance Survey only on its map of *Roman Britain* (1956). They were soon to be absent from its map of *Southern Britain in the Iron Age* (1962). To confuse matters, Crawford had hinted that his 'Celtic' fields might be a bit earlier than 500 BC, perhaps originating in what archaeologists called the Late Bronze Age (then about 750 BC) and therefore definitely pre-Celtic. This view was becoming increasingly attractive to Bowen as he wrote his book on the subject. He, and therefore I, initially suspected that, following more recent excavations on the Marlborough Downs showing some small cattle enclosures to be Late Bronze Age in date, our little enclosures on Fyfield Down, so similar in appearance, might be of a similar date. If excavation could show that to be correct, then we would have made a breakthrough, for the underlying fields could not be later than Late Bronze Age and might even be earlier.

That site was the start of a long search among the sarsens. Investigation of the enclosures at Wroughton Copse did not answer the 'Celtic' field question, however, so further exploration, survey and selective excavation became necessary. We set out not just to find sites and artefacts but to answer questions, primarily by fieldwork. Our basic question was always 'How does this landscape come to look like this ?' OK, it could be answered simply by saying 'because the sarsens have been cleared', but we wanted to know when that had occurred, for what reason, by whom and by what means. So we set out to find the places in the downland landscape where there appeared to be evidence available to answer such questions (**16**).

In the field we recorded, collected surface finds, surveyed, interpreted, squeezing the landscape for its evidence by direct observation of its surface features. Fieldwork was carried out for its own sake, but part of its purpose was to identify the 'critical points'

16 Fieldwork on Fyfield Down, here recording prehistoric fields which are probably of the later second millennium BC. This photograph is part of the record. In an area on the east of the Down expressing the essence of treelessness, the human figure and ranging pole mark the ends of the side of a prehistoric field picked out by daisies as much as by its bank or lynchet. This feature then turns at right angles across the front of the photograph to the standing stone on the extreme right before passing under the photographer, thus creating a stepped or staggered angle at the junction with the adjacent field. This is a characteristic feature of these fields, perhaps to give access between fields.

in that landscape. At such points, such as the figure-of-eight enclosure near Wroughton Copse, we attempted to establish crucial sequences by excavation. The far north end of Overton Down, as the following example shows, also proved to be one such point. From tiny excavations came enough evidence to hint that this particular local landscape had passed through a myriad of phases in its development and use.

Marks show up on the sarsens when the light is right. The first warden of the Fyfield Down National Nature Reserve was a retired archaeological professor, A.D. Lacaille. He showed us two of his discoveries, both first seen because of a growing familiarity with this place — and being in the right place at the right time. The discoveries were of workings on individual sarsen stones. In both cases we were able to place these stones in their landscape and in an archaeological context, converting them from curiosities into contributors to the history of these downs.

At the far northern end of Overton Down is a tongue of land next to the Ridgeway. It should, technically, be called 'Lockeridge Down', for it forms the northern extremity of the tithing of Lockeridge, but that estate has long since been subsumed within the modern parish of West Overton. Anyway, a cluster of quite large sarsens can be found there, in a small area of rough grazing, marked by rather straggly hawthorns, between a prehistoric ditch and a modern ploughed field. Search amongst the sarsens for the one which appears to be lying down, its long, flattish surface uppermost. This was the stone Lacaille led us to. Its surface is remarkable because it has been polished, so much so that a silica cortex has formed on it which glints in the sunlight. Indeed, it has been polished so much that a shallow dish-shaped hollow has been created. On the same stone are a series of roughly parallel grooves, just below the polished area (**24, colour plate 11**). Who on earth would do all this? And why? And why here, in this remote place high on the downs without a single habitation in sight?

But there is even more to this one sarsen. Closer inspection showed that along the edge facing the Ridgeway were some shallow, straight-sided notches. An explanation for this phenomenon at least seemed clear when it was realised that this westward-facing side had been relatively recently exposed. It had been formed by splitting away part of the polished stone. In other words, despite the remote location, the sarsen breakers had been here too and taken away a block of sarsen of unknown size and appearance. The notches along the edge of the remaining stone were where their wedges had been hammered into the sarsen to split it. There still remained, though, the questions of when this had occurred and what had produced the shining surface before us.

Probably ill-advisedly we decided to carry out a small excavation around the stone. Professor Lacaille's theory, and ours, was that the smooth upper surface was caused by the sarsen having been used as a workbench in the production of polished stone axe-heads. These are characteristic artefacts of Neolithic peoples hereabouts and date the polishing and sharpening to the fourth and third millennia BC. Most of the axe-heads were of exotic stone from Northern Ireland, the Lake District, Wales, Cornwall and, occasionally, Brittany. Our theory required the material to arrive in the form of rough-outs which were then worked up, perhaps to individual taste, into the beautiful objects (seldom used for chopping apparently), of the sort which now adorn Avebury, Devizes and Salisbury museums. Who knows, but a rough-out may have lain buried beside the sarsen? There should at least have been chippings, perhaps even a fragment of a half-polished axe-head in the exotic dark blue-stone of Preseli or the sleek green-stone of the Lakes.

What we actually found was an iron wedge. A few flint flakes indicated some human activity here either side of 2000 BC, but such material is widely spread across these downs. No chips of green or blue-stone, and certainly no rough-out, were found. So the theory of a Neolithic stone-axe workshop here was not substantiated, though the polishing of axe-heads on this sarsen remains the best explanation of the markings on its surface. The excavation, however, was able to place such activity in some sort of sequence. It showed that the stone had formerly been standing upright, so it was already an important stone before its use for axe-polishing (see *Aethelferthes* stone, **17a**).

Indeed, perhaps that was why, out of all the thousands of stones which could have been used, it was selected. Perhaps it was even pushed over for that purpose, a 'holy' menhir being converted to make sacred axe-heads. This is where its location could be so significant. It is right beside the Ridgeway which, although it did not come formally into existence until later Saxon times, could well have been an informal route 5000 years ago and earlier. Perhaps this stone, standing and recumbent, in some way marked the beginnings of a sacred landscape as approached from the north? — a landscape which, by the middle of the third millennium BC at latest, had apparently come to be centred on the great henge monument of Avebury, just over a mile (2km) downhill from Lockeridge Down. Our suggestion is no more than speculation, of course, but from such single stones do theories stem. At least the theory is inspired by some material evidence and the stone is so remarkable it demands some all-embracing explanation (and a visit).

17 'Mystery' sarsen stones on the downs. (a) Sarsen stone, part of the little concentration of similar stones including the polissoir at the north end of Lockeridge Down (fig **24**: this one is just north of 'p'). Though not of the usual proportions of a standing stone, this one does not appear to be naturally set but rather to be deliberately upright with its artificially-shaped, pointed top skywards. The East Overton charter of AD 939 refers to a stone of Aethelferthe at the northern end of the estate, and this may be it. The same name occurs near the southern boundary cf. **63**. (b) 'The Templars' Bath', Temple Bottom, Preshute, a large, tabular sarsen stone with a steep-sided hollow or trough cut into its upper surface, with a drain hole bored through the rock bottom right.

And let us not forget the much more prosaic iron wedge. It fitted the notches along the western edge where the missing block was split off, so here was the implement which so damaged our precious sarsen. Presumably it just slid to the bottom of the crack when the stone was split open and got lost in the ground disturbance as the departing block of sarsen was levered and dragged to the side. And when was this? The evidence this time was quite specific. Near the wedge was a half-penny — literally — of King John (1197-1206), so the stone was probably split a few years into the thirteenth century.

This almost bizarre conjunction of iron wedge, coin and split sarsen at the back of beyond at an apparently inconsequential date, found by chance in excavating something supposedly 4000 years earlier, actually has a simple and rational explanation, documentary rather than archaeological. It is one reason why we have re-instated Lockeridge Down on to the landscape. Lockeridge, from the mid-twelfth until the early fourteenth centuries, belonged in part to the Knights Templar. Their preceptory was high on the downs to the east near present day Wick Farm, only a mile (1.5km) distant from our sarsen (**46b**). And past the sarsen climbed one of the downland routes between Lockeridge village and the Templars' place, a route which followed a line entirely within the tithing of Lockeridge until it reached the Ridgeway. So the sarsen's situation and the date for its splitting, say in the decade up to 1210, are perfectly acceptable. With date, situation and context, not to say a little speculation, an interesting story emerged.

There is no known farm or the like nearby, so it is difficult to explain why this particular stone was split, when others around seem unaffected, and where its missing section was taken. Is there just a chance, we can at least muse, that the 'magical' nature of our sarsen was recognised, though not understood, by men of the knightly brotherhood who themselves were much concerned with the mysteries of belief and religion? Could they possibly have removed a part of it, perhaps also with markings on, to their lonely place of life and prayer on the downs? A possible interest in unusual stones going back to medieval times is hinted at by the remarkably curious, hollowed sarsen called 'The Templars' Bath' just over a mile (1.5km) away to the east in Temple Bottom. It is basically natural but it has had a shallow, bath-sized rectangular basin cut in its top, emptied through a two-inch (6cm) diameter, pentagonal drain cut or even drilled obliquely through the stone (**17b**). The explanation is probably mundane, a nineteenth-century horse-trough or bird-bath, but one wonders.

The other marked stone Lacaille took us to is on Totterdown, 770 yards (700m) east of the axe-polishing stone. This sarsen bears a cluster of several round depressions on its upper surface, each about two inches (6cm) across and each ground, somehow, into the stone. Technically these are called 'cup-marks', as they look like little cups and apart from examples in Cornwall, this is the southernmost example of them in England. These cup-marks are not much to look at, nevertheless, and the casual passer-by could well think them natural even if he or she noticed them at all. What they actually are, we just do not know, and why they are here, in the middle of a slight south-west facing slope strewn with sarsens, is a mystery. In north and west Britain, and elsewhere in Europe, they occur across a range from single ones to great works of rock art (**colour plate 12**).

To say that they are symbolic does not get us very far, but for those who knew some 4000 years ago they seem to have contained messages, perhaps about direction or land ownership or rites of passage. It is a megalithic code which we have not yet cracked. On Totterdown the cup-marked stone now sits towards the edge of a set of Roman arable fields, abandoned about 1800 years ago and which have been grass ever since. The stone's original context was probably in a Bronze Age landscape, though it might

18 Devil's Den, Clatford Bottom: a fanciful 1920s' restoration of a Neolithic chambered long barrow in the form of a 'cromlech', an antiquarian creation which did not exist in prehistory.

have stood in less regimented surroundings of scrub, pasture and cultivated patches in the third millennium BC. It is a very complicated field archaeology on the surface of Totterdown, especially on the wider view of an air photograph (**colour plate 25**). Yet fragments of arrangements which probably existed in the earlier second millennium BC when the landscape was beginning to be physically organised can be inferred. The stone may be a relic of even earlier times but it fits in comfortably with the landscape of 3800 years ago.

So a sarsen could be a tool, a guide, a boundary marker, as well as a readily available source of building stone. One of the other early ways in which sarsen was exploited was in the building of enormous tombs in the centuries leading up to about 3000 BC. These are known scientifically as megalithic or chambered long barrows. Such structures were for long the delight of antiquaries who, as creatures of their time, gave them heavily druidical names like 'cromlech' and 'dolmen'. Cromlechs, such as *Devil's Den* in Clatford Bottom, however, never existed until recently as the free-standing stone monuments you can see today. They are in fact merely the remains of a stone tomb (**18**). Originally the structure

19a Sarsens embedded in clay-with-flints scattered lightly over the highest, northern edge of Fyfield Down, abutting Clatford Down to the right. The slight ditch with its bank to the right up the centre of the picture is Fyfield's historical boundary with Clatford. The gorse bushes suggest a relatively acidic soil and the scrub indicates non-intensive land-use, as might be expected historically right on the edge of an estate. Not all the sarsens are in their natural position, for beneath the gorse is a burial mound with megalithic structure; on its south side is the millstone illustrated next. The trees on the skyline are in Totterdown Wood, half a mile (1km) north-west.

would have been covered by a mound, though this has subsequently been eroded, ploughed or sometimes actually quarried away. You can go and see a mound-covered long-barrow with its five internal burial chambers at the properly excavated and presented West Kennet long barrow, freely accessible by walking up a hill south from the A4 opposite Silbury Hill.

Because of their antiquarian attraction, many megalithic barrows were discovered, and often dug into, long before we arrived on the scene. We have scoured the downs for new examples and have found only one. It lies high on Fyfield Down in an area still of rough grazing and right beside the Ridgeway track coming south-east from Totterdown towards Manton (**19a**). We are not even sure that is a genuinely long one: it seems to be more oval, and may indeed be just a rather large round barrow of the early second millennium BC, a common type of burial place. That it is megalithic, however, is not in doubt, for large stones cluster around its centre. One looks as if it might be a capstone, that is the horizontal stone lid on top of the burial chamber. Another on its south side is, somewhat unexpectedly, a mill-stone; more correctly, an unfinished mill-stone (**19b**). You can see why it is still there: the mason made a mistake at a late stage in its preparation and had to abandon his work. Pretty sickening that, not just after hours of skilled work with difficult material but knowing that it is not that easy to find stones of the right material, thickness and rough shape for a big grinding stone.

Difficult too for us to guess accurately where the millstone's destination lay, for the other interesting thing about the barrow is that it is sited on a boundary, indeed several boundaries. It is never clear in such cases whether to draw the obvious deduction that clearly the boundary-makers used the earlier mound as a boundary-marker, something old which all interested parties could see and agree about, knowing that, unlike sarsen stones, it was not going to move. Though recognising the 'correct' interpretation on the basis of stratified physical evidence, that is to say the barrow lay at the edge of a field system and was constructed around 4000 years ago, one sometimes has the sneaking feeling that the barrow was placed where it was to be on a boundary that already existed. The boundary-makers of, for example, medieval times, would, if such were the case, merely be reinforcing an old line in the landscape as they dug the little bank and ditch of Overton Cow Down across the landscape up to and then over this burial place of the 'old ones'.

In fact, we found our 'new' megalithic barrow when we were following the parish boundary between Fyfield and modern Preshute, trekking uphill from 'Long Tom', a magnificent standing stone right on what is an ancient boundary still in use (**62**). Marked on the ground by a low bank and slight ditch on the Fyfield side, this boundary once divided the tithings of Fyfield and Clatford, so the millstone could have been intended for the mill at either village. But then it might equally have been destined for the manorial mill of East Overton, for the barrow is also skirted by that slight boundary defining Overton Cow Down (**64**). All three villages are of course on the River Kennet and it is not too tenuous to connect in the mind's eye the mills beside that source of

*19b Abandoned millstone, Fyfield Down: for precise position, see **19a**. This sarsen had perhaps been dragged out of the stone structure of the barrow mound (immediately left in this view) at the foot of which it lay, and was presumably being fashioned on this spot for use as the top stone of a pair of mill-stones. As is apparent, the grain of the sandstone did not, however, lend itself to circularity. The scale is extended to 100cm. For a smaller but successful Roman hand-mill stone, see **colour plate 22**.*

20 Discarded long barrow, Manton Down, as dumped in 1996 — the end (or just another phase?) of a long story of abuse of a chambered long barrow which was a Scheduled Ancient Monument supposedly protected by law; but it made the big mistake of being in the way of agricultural land improvement in the 1950s and has subsequently been totally destroyed. This presumably final resting place is about ¼–mile (c.400m) from the place where these stones were built into a tomb some 6000 years ago, a tomb which was respected by prehistoric farmers when cultivating their fields 2000-3000 years later. And 3000 years later again — progress? What progress?

power and the pathetically abandoned millstone, dragged out of a prehistoric barrow, 2½ miles (4km) away across the deserted downs. A mill has existed on the banks of the Kennet since the eleventh century, for Domesday tells us of a mill at West Overton paying 20s a year. Indeed, mills are recorded throughout the medieval period and right up to the early nineteenth century. The millstone could have been commissioned by a miller at any one of them.

All the megalithic long barrows on the downs have almost certainly been found. Our information about the number and distribution of such structures is therefore likely to be complete, a rare thing for a data-set in archaeology. Working in such detail in such a small area, however, can bring to light errors and misunderstandings in the existing record. We searched high and low for one particular sarsen-chambered long barrow on Manton Down, for example, because, as we discovered the hard way, a recent student placed it in the wrong place with his grid reference, somebody else had plotted its position wrongly on a map, and in recent land improvement it had been lifted bodily and dumped among some bushes. What was really confusing was that old Ordnance Survey maps showed it correctly in its original, Neolithic position — but how were we to know that? There is absolutely nothing to be seen there now (**20**).

A rather more visible confusion exists at the *Devil's Den*, the real site of a genuine megalithic long barrow in Clatford Bottom close to the tithing boundary with Fyfield.

After being recorded, it was virtually destroyed during the nineteenth century. Then a well-intentioned antiquary restored in just after the First World War, making it look like what he thought, in the climate of his time, it should look like. As a result we now have in the landscape a 1920s' cromlech on top of what remains of a genuine 5000-year-old tomb. The result looks fantastic but, however much it offends the megalithic purist, it is now effectively untouchable because it has become a much-valued part of the local heritage (**18**).

Devil's Den is of course a super name, as much a part of that heritage as the site itself. It is very much part of the attraction, mysterious and supposedly an example of unsophisticated peasants in days of yore attributing something they could not understand to the Devil. Indeed, they made the 'cromlech' his home, hence Devil's Den. We believe the derivation of the name, however, to be quite different. The Wiltshire agricultural tongue has garbled, twisted and simplified, probably only over the last two centuries, the much simpler, prettier and genuine name of *Dillion Dene*. Dillions are a little known phenomenon of downland landscapes. Most probably derived from the Old English *dælan*, meaning to divide or bestow, dillions are, as *The English Dialect Dictionary* of 1900 explains, 'earth-heaps to mark boundaries on the Downs'. On a map dated 1811, 'this part of the down [between Overton Cow Down and Fyfield Tenants Down] is divided by hills called Dillions'. The map-maker had dotted in dozens of small circles along the northern edge of the Valley of Stones down to Clatford Bottom. The division they mark is described in the AD 939 Saxon charter and in the 1567 Pembroke survey, so maybe the dillions have lain there, unnoticed and undisturbed, for 500, perhaps 1000 years.

We have in the meantime moved while searching among the sarsens to noticing tiny earthen mounds. Long time-scales and considerable complexities are already beginning to emerge so we need, as we discovered during our exploration, to look at this land more generally yet in even greater detail.

4

Looking at the land

People often ask us whether the downs were ever inhabited. They are puzzled by the apparent contradiction between their own sometimes scant knowledge of olden times, with schoolday memories of ancient Britons living on the hilltops, and the downs today, bare, dry and empty. Yet every now and then, they catch glimpses of former inhabitants: an upright stone, a barrow, a ruined barn, a disused chalk-pit. The downland landscape looks as if it might not just be a wilderness or merely an area of natural beauty, outstanding or otherwise. It has that look about it, as if it has been fashioned and then deserted. Nor is this sense of others before us ours alone. In the tenth century, a thousand years ago, we can detect too that the Anglo-Saxon boundary surveyors were also aware of ancestors in their landscape. They knew, for example, of the place where the heathen were buried and they gave names to prehistoric barrows. But if the downs were inhabited, where did the people get their water from? That is the question of perennial interest. Everybody knows you cannot live without water; so, since the downs are so dry now, they must have been different then. And, of course, they were; whenever 'then' was.

In this chapter and the next we try and find out where the downland inhabitants of the Land of Lettice Sweetapple worked and lived — and drew their water. Simple objectives, you would have thought, easily described and concluded. Not so, at least in our experience; though the water question, perhaps the most mysterious, is the easiest to deal with. Basically, as even limited travel outside Britain demonstrates to us and as our television pictures daily show, people without the convenience of tapped water do one or more of four things: they find a local source — a spring or well — they collect rainwater, they go and collect water from some non-local supply, and they take themselves and their animals to a distant supply. People living on our downs pursued all four options, for even up until today no-one has enjoyed water on tap there.

No downland springs exist locally now but it is extremely likely that, in days when there was a higher water table, water could have been obtained at certain points along the sides of the denes. Almost certainly this explains the long-lived popularity of the Pickledean Down Barn area — where we also know of underground, stone-lined channels best explained as water-conduits. We can guess with some assurance too that rainwater was assiduously collected, notably off roofs. Hints of this were obtained on a late prehistoric settlement (site OD XI) which we excavated high on the downs — what were frogs doing there for a start? — but in truth the evidence is always likely to be fugitive since wooden water butts and tree-trunk gutters do not leave much trace on dry-land sites.

The downs, however, are littered with other archaeological evidence; artificial ponds, evidence enough that rain was collected (we do not subscribe to the 'dew pond' school of thought). The most prominent, big square earthworks for watering livestock, are barely a century old, but there are many others, some definitely medieval (we excavated one which was part of a thirteenth-century farm in Wroughton Mead), some probably earlier. Collecting rainwater, especially from about 1000 BC onwards, probably adequately served

21 Map of the enclosed landscape of the downs, second millennium BC. This is a much simplified version of a detailed, large-scale map compiled from air photographs showing the field archaeology of Avebury, Overton, Fyfield and Manton Downs. It nevertheless indicates the extent of the systems of enclosed fields, their axial arrangements and the spatial relationship of some of the key sites to them. The letters A-M are labels for the round barrow cemeteries of the early/mid-second millennium. As far as is known, this map shows nothing later than c. 500 BC and the bulk of its content is certainly pre-1000 BC. Its grid is that of the National Grid at 1000m intervals.

domestic needs, but undoubtedly the main need, drinking-water for large numbers of livestock, was met by taking the horses, sheep and cattle to the water itself. Nowhere is the Kennet more than 2–3 miles (4km) distant from the downs in our parishes and a daily walk down to the river can be envisaged as part of the herdsmen's routine throughout the centuries. The 'problem' of water is one in our twentieth-century suburban minds rather than in the practicalities of pre-modern agrarian life.

The water question disposed of, our text can now become unashamedly discursive rather than following a rigidly logical progression; for that was in reality not only how we found 'things' but, rather more importantly, how over the years some sort of understanding of this place developed in our minds. Not only have we walked back and forth over these downs many times, learning something new on each occasion, but the

22 Overton, or Seven Barrow, Hill from the air, looking eastwards across the A4 and the Kennet towards West Overton village. Five of the barrows can be seen, including the very rare triple one in the middle. The group is typical in its position on the relatively high points around the edges of the western Marlborough Downs and Kennet valley, on the fringes of the enclosed prehistoric landscape. The small area shown in the foreground has witnessed three major changes since the photograph was taken, epitomising how new land-uses and new values are imposed, as usual in this area from outside. The track across the foreground is The Ridgeway, now a National Trail promoted by the Countryside Commission. The fields either side now belong to the National Trust. It has taken the field around the barrows out of cultivation to protect them from further physical damage; and its has removed the small shanty-town bottom right, including the much-revered Ridgeway transport café.

whole process of our trying to understand what has happened there, of how the landscape came by its present appearance has been, not along a straight line of progress but fitful, cumulative and serendipitous. So we have three aims here. First, we try to show how we set about finding the places where people worked and how they made a living on the downs. Second, and in the next chapter, we explore some of the places where they lived (we excavated three of them, so much can be said). Mixed up in our exploration of this landscape is our third aim: to look for the dead and their burial places, perhaps the most familiar bits of downland archaeology to those who just pass by. Who, after all, has not noticed that curious word *tumuli* on Ordnance Survey maps as they drive through Wiltshire or wondered at the mounds, sometimes beneath eye-catching clumps of beech trees, along the skylines and in the fields near Avebury (**22, 70**)?

As it happens, pursuing our first aim quickly elided with our third as a marked landscape relationship emerged between the living and the dead. In one respect, common sense tells us how people managed to gain a livelihood on the downs: they farmed. But we can be a little more refined than that, indicating different emphases in farming at different times and showing how and where some particular farming activities occurred. And, as we have already seen, farming was not the only economic activity on the downs: sarsens, for example, were also being used for building from early times and, more recently, recreation has become a factor.

Essentially, we found the ancients by looking for them, by searching for the places where they lived and worked and buried their dead. Their work-places were the easiest to find, precisely because the downland inhabitants were first and foremost farmers. But here the evidence we found was perhaps somewhat misleading in a subtle sort of way. Farmers work out in the open a lot of the time, cultivating their fields and looking after their stock which might or might not be kept in fields. We looked for and found ancient fields: not a very difficult task when their remains are so readily visible, especially on Fyfield Down and the west side of Overton Down (**25, colour plate 10**). However, we did rather more than look. We examined in detail, surveyed, and in some cases carried out, what were always intended to be small excavations. Perhaps above all, we gave the landscape time and simply came to know it well. This whole approach, involving in the end years of familiarisation, hundreds of miles of walking and surveying every 'old' feature in the landscape, culminated in a great map of the downs. Each surviving feature, whether a grass-covered earthwork, a soil-mark or a crop-mark in the modern arable, was plotted on to a map. Unfortunately, it is too large and detailed to be reproduced in this book, so we have to make do with a simplified, smaller-scale version of it (**21**). Our interpretations are based on the original, of course, for though the map itself is a marvellous record, it exhibits few self-evident truths. It has to be interpreted, just like the landscape itself.

23 Burial mounds and Jacob sheep, Overton Hill, perhaps as they might have appeared together in the later second millennium BC when an enclosed landscape of arable fields occupied much of the downs, leaving rough grazing around its fringes among the burial mounds of the ancestral cemeteries (cf. 22 and 70). This scene occurred in 1996 on the traditional pasture of The Cow Down in West Overton manor, an area cultivated between c.1960-90 but now returned to pasture for conservation reasons.

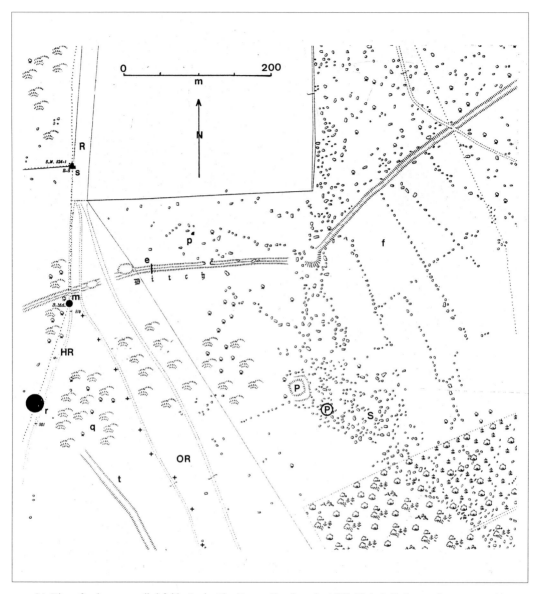

24 Plan of early stone-walled fields, Lockeridge Down. Based on the 1889 25 inch Ordnance Survey map, this adaptation retains some of the original cartography to show how the early surveyors actually measured in individual stones and recognised lines of stones which we would now see as the sides of fields of the first millennium BC. Here these early fields (f) relate to a long ditch across the landscape which appears to be a prehistoric boundary (it is the line between 'E' and 'Totterdown' on 21). The dotted line across it, top right, is the tithing boundary, now the parish boundary, between Lockeridge and, to the east, Fyfield. The line of small crosses along the track south eastwards from 'm' is the approximate position of the equivalent boundary between East Overton, on its west, and Lockeridge in AD 939. Other lettered features are: e excavation m boundary mound (dillion?) on the Anglo-Saxon boundary between East Overton and Avebury OR the route of the 'Overton Ridgeway' as described in the AD 939 East Overton charter P pond p polishing stone for Neolithic stone axes q quarry and spoil, partly overlying t R the present-day Ridgeway, formerly the Saxon 'herepath' (HR) r round barrow S sarsen stones at their densest at the head of the Valley of Stones s boundary stone at the junction of three Anglo-Saxon estates t a hollowed trackway, certainly of Roman date, if not earlier, and perhaps also either or both the 'Overton Ridgeway' and the Saxon estate boundary.

*25 Early fields, Totterdown, from the air, looking north-east across low, bright sunlight on a May evening. Bottom left is much the same area as **24** with lines of sarsen stones reflecting the light to show the early enclosed fields and their relationship to the boundary ditch heading up the slope towards Totterdown Wood. The scarp curving off the ditch before the Wood is interpreted as a remnant of a late prehistoric enclosure like site XI on Overton Down; it overlies the ditch. A Romano-British trackway a little to the right winds between the fields. Bottom right is the north east corner of Delling Wood, from which emerges the sharply-defined bank and ditch of a post-medieval enclosure cutting right across the early fields as it curves back to the left.*

The careful, patient plotting of each line showed up the edges of the fields criss-crossing their way across the land. Here was the evidence of how people had gained their livelihood in the past: they had ploughed the land and grown crops in hundreds of small enclosed fields stretching in a great swathe of countryside from near Avebury across to the Manton long barrow and, north to south, from a prehistoric boundary ditch on Totterdown almost to the River Kennet. This is an area roughly 5 miles (8km) by 4 miles (6.4km) (**21**).

The map may be a revelation to anyone unaccustomed to the idea of a whole landscape being a single archaeological site or to a visitor to the area seeing from the road just modern fields of wheat with no archaeology except an occasional round barrow. Even on the old grasslands of Fyfield and Overton Downs, where the humps and bumps become profuse, it is difficult for the walker to see any pattern. Yet the nature of this landscape is not so surprising, for such great extents of ancient landscapes have been archaeologically familiar since Crawford's original publications about them in the 1920s.

The map allows us a bird's eye view of the land. We are not looking, however, at a single landscape formed at one moment of time; rather are we looking at one which has developed through time, as you would expect if you think of how our landscape has changed in our

26 Excavated prehistoric field boundary, Fyfield Down: the stones in the section indicated where a low wall was positioned before its total removal at the end of the excavation. Behind it, some 5ft (1.5m) of accumulated soil was stratified in layers, with the dark brown soil at the bottom containing mainly Early/Middle Bronze Age material and early Roman pottery occurring among the large flints immediately under the topsoil. Collin Bowen and Geoffrey Dimbleby, who together inspired much of this research, ponder the evidence while it is recorded photographically by one of the authors as a young man, in August 1961.

own lifetimes, never mind about the historic changes over the last 300 years. Our map represents a composite evolved over 2000 years and more, roughly from 1800 BC to AD 400. The main phases can be picked out through a combination of geometrical analysis (looking for the patterns), sorting sites and earthworks into shapes and types (morphology and typology) and looking at the actual archaeology on the ground (fieldwork).

First of all, within the spaghetti-like lines on the map, there are three basic axes around which different sets of fields are aligned. Those axial lines are respectively 15½°, 46° and 7° west of true north. Each main axis is substantiated by lines at right angles to it, forming the corners of the fields. Judging by the the way in which different systems and indeed individual fields overlie one another in the landscape (stratigraphy), the field systems were laid out in the sequence just given for their axes, the 15½° set being the earliest, the 7° the latest.

The 15½° fields, arguably datable to the early/mid-second millennium BC, survive only fragmentarily for they have been ploughed over many times in the last 4000 years. They are best represented on eastern Fyfield Down and Manton Down, apparently related to a pair of round barrows and possibly to a long barrow on Manton Down. Other small areas of surviving fields in this layout occur north of Green Street on Overton Down. There they seem to have respected a superb surviving example of a saucer barrow. South of Green Street the fields respect barrow groups on Avebury Down. The suggestion is not just of a

27 Prehistoric field boundary, site Overton Down XI: the pegs in the foreground stand in post-holes, apparently of a fence against which ploughsoil in the field to the left accumulated, as seen in section. The soil contained only Early Iron Age material up to the layer with larger flints and chalk lumps immediately below the topsoil. That contained early Roman material. The large sarsens in the background characteristically sit in the top of that layer, marking the Roman fields in this area.

common axial arrangement over some three miles (5km) of downland but also of a close physical relationship with what are probably early round barrows. This reinforces the thought that this landscape is of the earlier second millennium, when elaboration of the basic mound and ditch shape of round barrows in Wessex was fashionable in ways exemplified on these downs. While we can observe that physical relationship, however, we can only guess at possible associations implied by it in the minds of those whose landscape this then was.

The 46° fields make up the bulk of the pattern on the map. On the whole their orientation goes with the grain of the countryside over much of the fields' extent so, even if it is not entirely natural, their layout was obviously strongly influenced by the topography. Yet it is nevertheless deliberate, this north-west to south-east axis, for it is closely consistent over eight square miles (20 km^2) of varying terrain, resulting in parts of the arrangement lying awkwardly in relation to the ground. Indeed, in some parts the need to conform unquestioningly to this axis leads to some peculiar field arrangements. This is at its most impressive when looking at the field edges which shoot off at right angles to the axis. The master plan — and why should we not think of such? — required arrangements of fields and tracks to conform blindly uphill, down slope and across valleys on a 134° axis from the top of Fyfield Down almost as far as the barrows overlooking West Kennet, a distance of almost two miles (3.5km). Surely it is easier to plough a field whose edge follows the top of a valley, rather than cut right across the valley? In some places large areas are not intervisible: you cannot, for example, see Fyfield Down from the south-west facing slopes of Overton Down, yet the same axis governs the layout of fields and tracks on both.

28 Three modern fence-posts have been set for visual effect in three of the post-holes marking the prehistoric field boundary on site Overton Down XI (27).

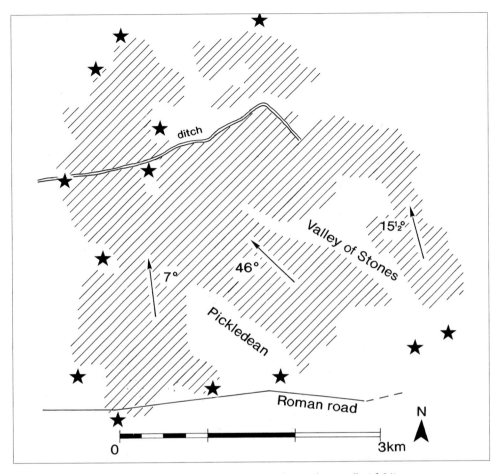

29 *Map of barrow groups and prehistoric fields on the downs shown schematically (cf. 21).*

Key: *The hatched area is the enclosed landscape of the second millennium BC, with arrows indicating its three main axes. The suggestion is that 15½° is the earliest and 46° the main one; 7° is Roman. The stars represent the barrow groups (A-M on 21), effectively the Early/Middle Bronze Age cemeteries, suggestively spaced around the rim of the downs and always on the edge of the enclosed landscape.*

When the earlier system (15½°) was abandoned, it was apparently replaced by this large-scale reorganisation around 1500 to 1000 BC. Our belief is that this new system was, at least in part, a reaction to erosion produced by intensified farming in a warm and dry climate. The previous centuries of ploughing previously uncultivated land had led to serious soil drift, helped by hot spells, warm winds and sudden downpours. The people, naturally, wanted to keep their living on the downs, so they had to reorganise their land systematically and edge their fields to stop the erosion. To do this they dug ditches or built fences, walls or banks along the sides of the fields. Though they also marked the field boundaries, their other purpose was to stop the ploughsoil slipping away. Over time the soil accumulated behind those permanent field boundaries and created earthen scarps like steps up and down the slopes. These are what the lines on our map represent. We call them lynchets, and have been doing so ever since our Anglo-Saxon forebears named them 'hlinc'. Often made even higher because ploughing also removed soil from their lower edges, they stand up to 10 feet (3m) high on both Fyfield and Overton Downs (**26, colour plate 6**). Visitors find it difficult to believe that they have not been built, like the ramparts of a hillfort, but essentially they represent slow soil accumulation against the boundary at the lower end of a cultivated field. We cut a section through one of the largest lynchets of Fyfield Down, showing exactly that.

The map shows not just ancient fields but other elements which existed physically in the contemporary landscapes. On it, as on the ground, are elements of pre-modern systems of trackways running between the fields. Clearly, they provided the means to move herds and flocks through this organised landscape, and they also led out of it, apparently for two main purposes. They gave out on to apparently empty spaces, at least in the sense that there is no visible archaeology. In other words, they led to pasture-land, invisibly as important and probably as planned an element in a landscape of mixed farming as the more obvious enclosed fields for cereal crops such as wheat and barley (**23**).

This peripheral land was also where at least some of the dead were buried, for here were grouped the round burial mounds. These were quite different from the long barrows we searched for among the sarsens for, in addition to their different shape and size, they were built in general over single, rather than communal, burials, characterising the period around 2000 BC and later. And since the barrows seem to be part of this functionally organised landscape, they are probably pointing us towards the sort of date at which the field systems and trackways were in use. Therefore, it is difficult to avoid the inference that we are looking at a landscape of 3000-4000 years ago. So the original name for the 'Celtic' fields really was mistaken for, even if Celtic peoples did invade Britain across the Channel in significant numbers about 2600 years ago, the great field systems across Avebury, Overton, Fyfield and Manton Downs clearly belong to a time some 500-1000 years earlier (**25–8, colour plate 13–4**).

The clear association in the landscape between fields, tracks and groups of round barrows suggests intensive farming with a premium on space in a countryside organised for production and efficiency. This inference might well suggest a relatively high population, but whether it was governed by a local strongman, an oligarchy or in democratic fashion is impossible to say. The contents of the barrows, especially now we can see their relationship to the working landscape, hint that around, say, 1600 BC, the second option might be the most plausible interpretation.

The map is also a splendid basis for playing archaeological games, some seriously, in that they apparently help us to understand what was going on here 3000-4000 years ago. Let us, for example, stay with the round barrows. There are hardly any single ones or pairs; the great majority are in clusters or groups of three or more (the largest cemetery contains about 15 barrows). Not uncharacteristically for the Wessex chalklands, these groups are typically situated on high ground, often on local bluffs or spurs. Impressively puncturing the skyline, they were apparently meant to be seen from below (**12**). Whatever the meaning or significance of their situation, there can be no real doubt that those who built the barrows deliberately sought out places in the locality where they would be prominent. Maybe this was so that the old ones could keep an eye on the living, a useful story to put about by those exercising local authority and with a vested interest in keeping things that way. Even so, it was not worth giving up the best farming land for the purpose when such a social mechanism could just as well, and even better, be operated from on high around the edges of the farmlands. Then the spirits of the dead could invisibly survey the fields of the workers on the downs as well as look out over whatever was going on along the valley sides and river banks and, of course, take note. The installation of television cameras for surveillance of our city streets may not be such a novel idea after all.

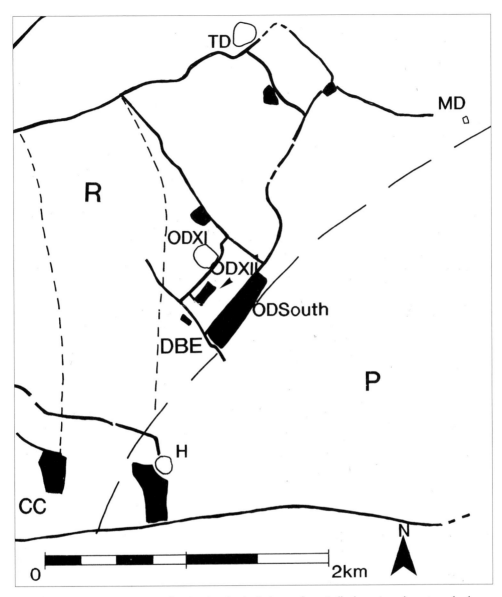

30 *This map tries to present a complex situation simply. It shows schematically the main settlements on the downs from 'CC' to 'MD' (see* **Key** *below), linked by the later prehistoric/Roman track system. All survive as earthworks except 'CC' and 'MD' which have recently been ploughed over, and 'H' which has been under cultivation for a thousand years plus and is only known from cropmarks (36). They are plotted against two zones, one, 'P', the area of permanent arable in which no settlements are known except 'H'; the other 'R', representing the area cultivated in the early Roman period which, although now mainly grass, contains no earthwork settlements and, being grass, no cropmarks settlements either — except 'H' at its southern limit. The implication is clearly that settlement remains as we have located them are not so much the product of where people lived as of land-use after the settlements' desertion.*

Key: *Open symbols: later prehistoric. Solid black symbols: Romano-British. CC 'Crawford's complex' DBE Down Barn Enclosure H Headlands MD Manton Down Bronze Age enclosure OD XI site Overton Down XI OD XII site Overton Down XII OD South Overton Down South settlement P permanent arable R Roman arable TD Totterdown later prehistoric settlement.*

Another correlation becomes apparent on our schematic map (**29**), this time between the barrow groups themselves. They are spaced out not merely topographically but also metrically, at least in a rough and ready sort of way. The groups lie almost equidistant from each other, about half a mile (800m) apart, around the south-western rim of the Marlborough Downs. The anomalies in this pattern stand out. Clearly, for example, a group is missing north of the south-western one; while the gap on line between Pickledean and the Valley of Stones groups is already beginning to be filled. Doubtless further fieldwork and air photography will convert the pair of barrows already known there into a full-blown group in due course. The map, then, is not only a record; it is also a predictive as well as an interpretive tool.

It does not, however, explain the complete absence of barrow groups along the eastern side of our ancient landscape. This may reflect a lack of suitable prominent places but there could be more to it than that. The landscape of prehistoric enclosure comes to a definite end across Clatford and Manton Downs, but there is no topographical reason for this to be so. The downland continues eastwards, so there is plenty of room for a landscape of organised exploitation to expand further. But it does not. Such negativism reinforces our theory that fields and barrow groups went together, in both their presences and their absences.

These extensive landscapes of enclosure across our downs represented a major capital investment by those farming communities of 3000-4000 years ago. No barbarians these, they knew exactly what they were doing. Their achievement was to create and sustain a reasonably reliable mechanism to feed themselves by their own efforts at a time of growing population. This pragmatic approach seems to contrast markedly with the previous millennium. Then an increasing amount of social effort in the Avebury area seems to have been invested in ever more and bigger ceremonial monuments. It was not just the physical labour that is so striking: if you have enough manual workers, you can build banks and ditches and mounds almost as large as you want. It is the absorption of resources overall, the likely social disruption and the certain diversion of effort from the less glamorous tasks of the immutable agrarian cycle which impress us. Certainly Avebury henge, the West Kennet Avenue, Silbury Hill, The Sanctuary on Overton Hill and the great palisaded enclosures by the Kennet river, as well as other resource absorbing monuments built apparently over only a few centuries some 4500 years ago, represent a huge achievement, and doubtless the gods were pleased; but who was back at the farm mucking out the byre, weeding the fields and actually producing food? We suspect that the answer is 'not as many or as often as good husbandry requires'. And that ultimately obsessional monumentality induced a crisis, a systems collapse. Which brings us back to our fields on the downs, the rational reaction to a calamity. They are a remarkable fact. This agrarian master landscape on the downs of the second millennium BC is a direct result of the visually more spectacular, but ultimately pointless and wasteful sacred landscape of the third millennium.

Ultimately, however, agrarian pragmatism also failed, for by 500 BC the downs lay agriculturally exhausted and wetter winds whistled over abandoned arable fields. No-one seems to have lived here then: we have not found a single habitation from the five centuries before the Roman invasion. The grass which we now see, that sward which we now so prize that it contributed to the designation of the Fyfield Down National Nature Reserve, developed during these later prehistoric centuries, doubtless helped by sheep and perhaps horses as the downs reverted to their long-term, proper use as pasture. So in one sense the sward on our Downs is old grassland, but it is only 2500 years in age, and that is not of great antiquity when set against the lengthy history of this place.

A clutch of unusual details which came to light in excavations on Overton Down (Site ODXI; see Chapter 5) bears on these wider points. We found over an area of about 1400 square yards (1400m^2) slightly wobbly grooves scored into the surface of the chalk bedrock. These had been made by little wooden ploughs, technically called ards, as they were dragged backwards and forwards across the squareish fields. The plough-marks were parallel and about 30in (90cm) apart. Then the process was repeated at right angles to their first alignment, creating a chequered pattern in the chalk. In this way, as modern experiment has shown, they were able to churn up the soil fairly effectively. The wear on a wooden share-point cutting through even the light soil and, occasionally, the crumbly surface of the bedrock of Overton Down would have been tremendous, so the tip of the share was protected by fitting it with a cap. We found such a cap in our area of ard-marks, an iron one so probably of early Roman date. We were also able to see the 10ft (3m) headland, between the edge of the ploughing and the edge of the field, on which the ploughman turned the two-ox team which pulled the ard.

That is a scene which, with minor differences, would have been familiar on the downs any time from the fourth millennium BC until well into the early medieval period. The downs experienced another brief phase of cultivation in the first two centuries AD. We had identified one discrete field system on Totterdown during fieldwork in the early days: it was quite different in its appearance from the familiar prehistoric fields. We made a plan of it in 1964 and then excavated some minor, tactically placed cuttings into it in 1965 (**colour plate 4**). They showed beyond reasonable doubt that these fields were under cultivation around AD 100, so it was not entirely surprising to find this activity had been more widespread, primarily across Overton Down where it is represented by the '7° field system'.

Its field edges run almost exactly north to south on today's magnetic compass. More significantly, however, it is exactly at right angles to the west-east alignment of the Roman road which ran from Silbury Hill along the east slope of Overton Hill and down into Fyfield. This is a seriously Roman field system, not centuriation but an area of high ground laid out metrically to encompass about 315 acres (125 ha) of Overton Down north from the road. This system consisted of embanked, oblong fields characteristically 110 yards (100m) long, or longer, by some 45–50 yards (40–50m) wide. Their length:width ratio ranges from 2:1 to 5:1. These are quite distinct from prehistoric, and indeed medieval, fields, so they and their system would stand out anyway.

Other long fields on the downs (shown on a separate map, **41**) appear related to estate boundaries and occur, we think, where landowners, not surveyors, deemed they should occur. These are made up of 'ridge and furrow', or 'broad rig' as it is sometimes called. Such represent the fossilised remains of medieval ploughed fields, here peripheral to the great, permanent open fields of the medieval manors on the valley sides. These downland cultivation ridges are everywhere slight, long, low and slightly sinuous undulations on the surface of the ground, rather like wide, worn corduroy on a pair of trousers.

The best example shows very well on the air photograph of Fyfield Down (**colour plate 10**), where the ridge and furrow is associated with an excavated medieval settlement (see Chapter 5) and is probably thirteenth century. Some ridge and furrow on the downs is a little earlier and some no doubt later, but most, we believe, dates from the 1200s. It represents in the landscape the demand of a growing population and an expanding economy which forced agriculture to exploit its resources to the limits. It had to intensify and to expand outwards within the manorial lands, which often meant upwards too. What we are looking at, therefore, is the archaeological evidence for the ploughing up for a brief period of old grassland on the estate margins. The situation of most of these patches of cultivation close to the tithing boundaries is no accident, but it is nevertheless striking how well the cultivators respected, and therefore knew about, old boundaries now meaningless to us. The tithings of West Overton, East Overton and Lockeridge, now all in the modern parish of West Overton, and the similar tithings of Fyfield and Clatford to the east, provided the tenurial framework for this arable expansion. The only boundary significantly crossed was that between Lockeridge and Fyfield, both run as part of the manor of East Overton for much of the medieval period (**colour plate 15**).

This archaeological evidence of arable farming on the downs 700 years ago must not, however, distract us from what was really going on there at the time. Before, during and after this arable march to the margins, sheep farming dominated. Unfortunately, sheep farming, by its very nature, leaves little archaeological trace on the landscape — except 'old grassland' (see **68**). But, as we know from documents, there were 'sheepcotes', places where shepherds gathered with their flocks for shelter, feeding and lambing (the squares on **41**); some became habitations. One such was Raddon (R on **41**), and we guess another was where The Beeches (B) were later planted, for thirteenth-century occupation material has turned up there too. The other documented sheepcotes in East Overton and Lockeridge we show located at earthwork enclosures, post-Roman but otherwise undated (2 and 3). Number 1 in West Overton tithing we locate not on the basis of archaeological evidence but at a place marked 'Penning' on eighteenth-century maps.

It is perfectly obvious that we had to look hard for places where people actually lived, but we found some; people did actually live on the downs, sometimes.

5

Dwelling on the downs

Early habitation sites on the downs proved progressively more difficult to recognise the further we went back in time. Indeed the earliest, our only downland Mesolithic settlement site and about 7000 years old, was invisible because it was buried under more than 4ft (1.2m) of what had been mud. 'Settlement' is the word that archaeologists like to use for a place where people lived because it is neutral, with no commitment as to whether it is a city or a single hut or how long the place was occupied. This Mesolithic settlement, situated near Down Barn in Pickledean, typically provides barely a clue as to what once was, and raises lots of questions about where and in what people lived on the downs over the nine millennia between 10,000 and 1000 BC. The trouble is most settlement sites are of several phases, sometimes in different periods: this Mesolithic settlement, for example, was in the lowest of four main layers spanning some 5500 years in their formation. So the task is not quite as simple as it might sound, though that should not deter anyone from facing up to the complexity that is the nature of settlement archaeology.

31 Down Barn enclosure from the air, looking south east across Pickledean towards Down Barn. It had a low bank and slight ditch, enclosing a trapezoidal area with a low platform along the far side. The patch of nettles at its eastern end to the left marks a pond. To its left, the enclosure ditch clearly cuts the ledge along the dene-side, part of the Romano-British track system on Overton Down. We suggest that the site is the 'missing' Hackpen sheep-cote, perhaps of Saxon date. Much of the detail of the site has now been smoothed over but it still exists as excavation showed in 1995.

The earliest settlers did not live on the downs, not because they lived only elsewhere but because the downs did not exist. The hills and slopes and valleys were there of course, but they were clothed in post-glacial forest, not grass, a situation which persisted in general to about 5000 BC. Thereafter the forest was gradually cleared, but the early inhabitants camping near Down Barn in the little valley now called Pickledean would not then have been surrounded by treeless downland. Their environment would have been forest, perhaps not unlike parts of Savernake Forest today, with big oaks and beech, a little understorey beneath the leafy canopy, as well as natural glades and possibly the occasional clearing. Their Down Barn site may have been in such a clearing in a sheltered spot, probably near the water which then lay, at least sometimes, along the bottom of the dene. We cannot say much about the settlement itself because it was only glimpsed at the end of an excavation of a much later site, but a few flints and a pit or large post-hole were discovered in a soil layer immediately on top of chalk bedrock, itself sealed by a Neolithic layer with Bronze Age, Roman and post-Roman layers above that. Though perhaps as many as 2000 years later, the small amount of Neolithic material is itself a rare occurrence on these downs of evidence of occupation at that date. Given that there was later occupation of the site too, clearly the Down Barn area has been a favourite one through the ages. Indeed, it is one of what we came to recognise as 'nodal points' in the landscape (**31**).

But we must not be misled by the archaeology: it may be the only Mesolithic settlement we found but it would certainly not be the only one to have existed. Its position and later burial beneath soil deposits give us the clues: other places where people lived hereabouts, generally over the thousands of years up to about 2000 BC, are also likely to have been sited in sheltered places close to water in and along the sides of the small valleys. Such sites are now invisible and difficult to find because, as the landscape has evolved over the last 4000 years, especially under the impact of farming, they have become buried, broken up and dispersed by movement of soil and water. We are so accustomed to a calm and peaceful countryside in southern England that we forget the long slow changes taking place beneath our feet all the time, and have little experience of the dramatic soil moving effects of, for example, a flash-flood. All that said, unlike the soil, we must not get carried away. It is unlikely that at any one time before, say, 4000 BC, there were more than a few small groups of people living on what are now the downs. Camping is a better word, for the chalk uplands were probably primarily a summer and autumn hunting zone for people who killed and collected but then moved on and did not stay to farm.

Archaeologists have been trying for decades to find the living places of the people who built Avebury and its sacred landscape of about 3000-2000 BC, but without much success. These downs contribute little to this puzzle. The local inhabitants were certainly farming by then (the Neolithic) but they too trod lightly on the earth in terms of where they lived. These people are just so elusive domestically, almost as if they lived only through their monuments. Most unsatisfactorily, we are left to infer that they probably did not settle in permanent habitations and that, while they could put up great megalithic long barrows and long stone rows, they simply did not build in stone for their daily lives (not here, anyway, though they did elsewhere in England). Nor, apparently, unlike their ancestors in Europe, did they use their undoubted knowledge of wood technology to build themselves massive timber halls. As a result, the places where they lived have left no obvious impact or even trace upon the downland landscape. There just do not seem to be the low embankments, hut circles and house platforms, so familiar of later times, for us to find. That is not to say that these structures were never scattered across the downs. Clearly, on parts of the chalk uplands the surfaces on which

32 Excavation, Down Barn enclosure 1995: a trench north-south right across the enclosure in the 1960s was re-emptied. It showed that the earthwork was the last of a long sequence of events which began with activity here in this shallow valley some 8000 years ago. The earthwork in fact sits on four clearly stratified layers visible in the photograph, especially to the right of the figure. The flecked layer between the thick deposit of soil and the topsoil was full of Roman material sealed by the bank of the enclosure. The environmental evidence from this long sequence in the middle of the downs could be especially useful, and here Colin Shell of Cambridge University is taking soil samples.

people lived 5000 years ago have disappeared, weathered away by wind and rain and chemical action on the chalk. With it has gone the vast majority of the structural evidence for Neolithic settlement (**32**).

Still, we do find some things, sometimes just below the modern ground surface, sometimes beneath later soil accumulation or a structure. The finds tend to be flints, sherds of pottery or an occasional small pit or posthole, at best in a dark soil with charcoal and perhaps a broken piece of non-local stone and the empty shell of a hazelnut. Not exactly gripping stuff but that is how it is. Flint flakes, generally of Neolithic or Bronze Age types, occur almost ubiquitously on the downs and to the south along the edges of West Woods, so people were clearly around. At one or two places concentrations of such flakes have suggested actual knapping sites, where a few people stayed awhile to fashion flint scrapers and arrowheads.

The Sanctuary, that great monument on Overton Hill, may hide a clue to where people were living — though like all clues it may mislead. When The Sanctuary was in use, all sorts of material was deposited in it, presumably as part of a ritual. Though the structure faces west along the West Kennet Avenue, most of this material, the pots, stones and animal corpses, strongly points to the east and north as the directions from where the deposits were brought, suggesting a sort of back door. Doubtless long-distance travellers were among those who entered the sacred place by the back door, as it were, but it is also a pleasant thought that local people living on the eastern slopes of Overton Hill or to the north-east along Pickledean below Overton Down popped in from that eastern side for a quick deposit every now and then. It tells us something of the sanctity of the place, incidentally, that close on that same north-eastern side a barrow cemetery developed during the next millennium in a tradition revived a thousand years later by a row of Roman barrows and a pagan Anglo-Saxon cemetery. Some would see the nearby, mid-twentieth-century transport café, now sadly also deceased, in the same tradition.

Frustrating though the settlement archaeology is from 4000 to 2000 BC, and there is no alternative, it hardly improves for the next millennium (the Bronze Age). We may now have extensive, organised landscapes spread across the landscape of Fyfield and Overton Downs (see Chapter 4), but there is precious little evidence of where the farmers actually lived. In fact, the record is pitiful. All we have for certain on our downs is a small enclosure among the prehistoric fields on Manton Down and an excavated fragment of a settlement of about 900 BC on Overton Down. These would give a total downland population, even over 500 years (1500 to 1000 BC), so small as to be uncountable, which is clearly nonsense with so many hectares under plough and managed pasture. Where are the missing thousands of people of the third millennium BC to put up those great monuments, never mind about those of the second millennium to manage these great landscapes? Clearly there is a mismatch here, between what must have been and the evidence that we have accumulated. So either the people lived elsewhere or there are lots of downland settlements we have not found, although both these notions are possible (**30**).

Perhaps the places where people lived are now deeply buried under eroded soils, ploughed flat or covered over by later structures. That is why we have not found many. There is plenty of food for thought there, not least because we repeatedly found evidence of activity earlier than that which we had set out to examine whenever we carried out an excavation. Maybe the permanent settlements of our Bronze Age farmers were elsewhere, not on the downs at all. They could have lain along the bottom of the valley slopes in places where either later cultivation has rubbed them out or they have become covered by eroded soils. There is now plentiful evidence from elsewhere, not least along the lower reaches of the Kennet and the Thames, that people were living and were very busy in the valleys. So by about 1000 BC it seems people had moved down to the Kennet, leaving the downs to become a bit of a backwater.

The site we unglamorously labelled ODXI was never going to solve the settlement problem but at least it was a real settlement, lived in over just two or three centuries, perhaps even less, round about 700 BC. It lay towards the top of the south west facing slope of Overton Down and we ended up excavating something over 10,000 sq. ft ($300m^2$) of it. We found it by examining an air photograph taken by Crawford and published in 1928. We were, as usual, really looking for places where we might be able to date ancient fields and in this respect this old photograph was particularly promising. It showed the familiar fragmentary, rectilinear pattern of ancient fields on Overton Down, but on this one particular photo, a curved bank or lynchet stuck out like a sore thumb among the straight lines. We wondered if that curve in the landscape was the relic of an embanked enclosure around a settlement which had since been largely destroyed by the fields which overlay it. If so, then here we might have another chance. It was relatively easy, so the argument went, to date a settlement. Therefore, by dating a settlement sandwiched between two plough soils, we could acquire a date by which the fields had gone out of use and probably, at the same time, be able roughly to date the fields which overlay the settlement.

Well, the theory was fine, and at its core the basic idea stood the test of prolonged and quite detailed excavation. We did date the settlement and we did, in a funny sort of way, date the fields. The archaeological reality was, however, much more complex, as had been the events here in the past, and all of it on a site where a mere 10in (25cm) lay between the present grass and the chalk bedrock. Yet between the chalk and the grass we detected fifteen phases in eight main periods of activity over about 3940 years, from 2000 BC to AD 1940. Those phases illustrate what can be squeezed into, and scientifically out of, the thin soils on the Upper Chalk below old grassland. You might care to ponder, nevertheless, how much disruption of this fragile evidence, of relationships much more than things, just one pass by a tractor with a modern eight-furrow plough would cause.

We shall just look briefly at the settlement phases here, but we cannot ignore altogether either our beginning or our end. Presumably it was just coincidence that soon after the start of our excavation of a settlement we should encounter a small cemetery occupying the same spot about 1200 years earlier than the settlement. We excavated three graves, two superimposed with complete skeletons in them, and another a few feet away which had been sliced through by a pit. The prehistoric pit-diggers had removed the whole of that third skeleton neatly down to the knees, leaving us with the lower legs and feet. Whether the other bits and pieces of human bone we found over the site came from this one disturbed burial, or from other graves in the vicinity, we do not know, but we suspect the cemetery was larger (**colour plate 16**).

These were the only skeletons we found throughout the project so, in a sense, these are the only actual people we met on the downs from prehistoric times. One was an apparently healthy child about seven years old, with no abnormalities or signs of disease. It had been buried first, head to south, facing east, knees flexed and with a complete and unique Beaker pot on its chest (**colour plate 31**). Partly over its grave was that of a well-built male in his twenties, 5ft 7in (1.7m) tall, head to the east, facing south, knees flexed and with sarsen 'cushions', patches of small stones, beneath his head and ankles. He had no possessions but his corpse had been surrounded by an oval of flints. He had suffered from dental problems. The one we only knew from below the knees was probably female, an adult 5ft 4in (1.6m) tall and with no health problems in her lower regions. She too had been buried head to south, facing east and with her knees flexed. We know them in death and obviously wonder if they were father, mother and child in life. If only we knew where they lived; surely it cannot have been far away.

When people began inhabiting this spot seriously, soon after 1000 BC, they were probably unaware they were living on a cemetery. But we wonder: was it not a little suspicious that these three Beaker graves, already perhaps 1000 years old, lay in an open area between successive Iron Age buildings (b and a on **34**). All the main buildings were circular and we excavated four of them completely. It would be nice to imagine a hamlet

33 Excavation, late prehistoric settlement, site Overton Down XI: features sealed beneath the lynchet of a prehistoric field (just visible in section top left) showing up in plan as dark soil fillings in the surface of the chalk bedrock before they were excavated. The ranging pole lies across the western arc of the foundation trench of building 'b' in **34a** *as it cuts through the tops of three pits, viewed from the north.*

of these thatched round houses with smoke wisping its way from their conical peaks, but unfortunately for that familiar, cosy picture of the Ancient Brits at home, probably only one such home was ever standing at one time.

The earliest building was a bit conjectural, for we only happened to come across it while excavating a lynchet and only saw an arc of its wall (so we have not shown it on **34a**). This wall was represented by postholes cut into the chalk bedrock. Into the slots went the wooden uprights on to which the framework of a timber wall was built. The building seemed to be standing in the corner of a field within the Overton Down system, suggesting that someone had the bright idea of using the already existing, slightly platformed and embanked area of a field as a settlement enclosure. This is an idea which seems to have been used elsewhere at some of the few Bronze Age settlements we can actually identify by their earthworks on the Marlborough Downs.

The idea caught on at Overton Down, for a new phase of occupation began. Four buildings (a-d, **34a**) were placed close together, probably successively. The first (a) was constructed quite differently from the earlier one under the lynchet. It was built, not by digging a separate hole for each wall post, but by digging a continuous trench into which posts were set and then banged firmly in place (**33**). Why this different construction technique was adopted we do not know; perhaps it was a change brought in by new people or by just one trendy, travelling builder. Perhaps it was of no significance at all. In any case it would hardly have made the houses look any different — if they were just single, round buildings. But Building 'a' was not like that.

Its construction seems to have marked some sort of break with the past and set the

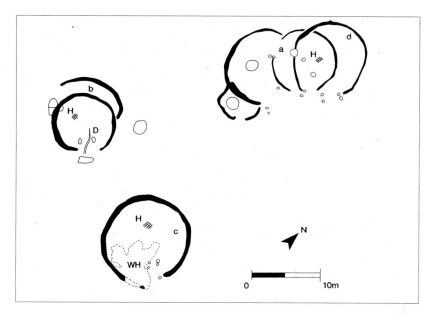

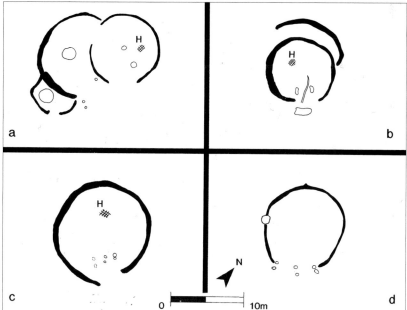

34 Plans of late prehistoric buildings on site Overton Down XI.

(a) *The cluster of buildings as excavated, in their correct spatial relationship.*

(b) *The buildings separated out into individual structures arranged in a chronological sequence a–d.
If the interpretation of 'a' as the earliest is correct, then the sequence develops from complex to
simple, at least in terms of plan.*

Key: *a the earliest, tripartite structure; b the second, bipartite structure; c a single cell round
structure; d a sub-circular structure with no hearth and wide entrance; D drain; H hearth; WH
'working hollows'. The larger open circles are pits, the smaller ones post-holes.*

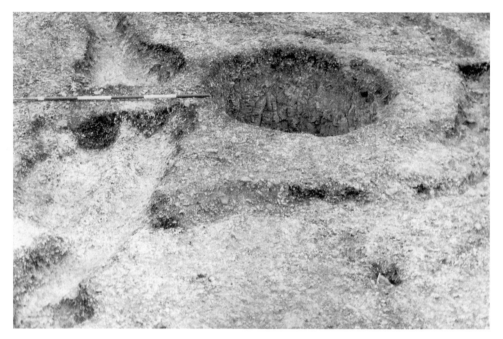

*35 Excavation, late prehistoric settlement, site Overton Down XI: detail after excavation of the southern arc of the foundation trench of the central part of structure 'a' in **34a** viewed from the west, with the similar trench of the small southerly annexe containing the pit illustrated in **colour plate 18.***

tradition for the three succeeding houses (b, c, d). Structurally, it began as a round house with entrance. To it a C-shaped and larger structure containing a pit was added on the south west, and on to the south of that was attached a small D-shaped annexe (**colour plate 17**). This possessed it own doorway and contained a large pit with a fine dark brown sediment horizontally across its bottom (**colour plate 28**). Our favoured interpretation is, then, that the inhabitants ended up with a rather impressive three part building. On the east was the circular living room with its hearth and typically south eastern, rather grand double-leaf doorway. In the centre, with an internal interconnecting doorway, the large room contained a big central pit with a ritual deposit of knives and ox-skulls, presumably the household shrine but also large enough for pragmatic people to use for storage or even for stalling the animals such as their ox plough-team. Stuck on the outside, tucked away behind the external entrance and with its own external, person-sized doorway (4ft; 1.2m), was the earth closet (**35**).

Now it seems that another big change came, this time changing not the building type but the settlement form. A new, purpose-built bank and ditch was constructed to form a 400-yard (360m) protective perimeter around the living area. In it Building 'b' was put up next, 83ft (25m) west of Building 'a'. This new home implies that the grand, three-roomed house had now been replaced by something simpler in plan. Building 'b' was a round house of about the same diameter and style as Building 'a', but now with only a single, smaller annexe, this time on the north. We called it 'the bicycle shed' as its shape came to light during excavation and probably that idea is essentially correct. That is, it could have been the all-purpose shed in which things are put which are not allowed in the house, though we suspect it was primarily where cattle were stalled, particularly as a pattern of postholes immediately on its north west might mark the foundations of an above ground, wooden grain store of a type (in stone) still in use in Galicia, Spain.

That leaves us with two buildings, 'c' and 'd', some 30 yards (30m) apart and both later than the previous ones, judging by their associated finds. They are, however, impossible to separate one from the other in time. They may indeed have formed a contemporary pair, with Building 'c' as the house with its standard hearth and south-eastern doorway, but now no annexe at all, and Building 'd', standing on the other side of the farmyard, serving other, non-domestic purposes. Building 'd' is a somewhat different building anyway. It had no hearth, a very wide, double-leaf doorway, as of a barn, a marked cluster of postholes and stakeholes outside its entrance as if in a working and/or tethering area. Furthermore, it seems to have been ritually 'killed', for an elaborate deposit of bones and artefacts had been placed on the line of its western wall in the top of a pit which had been deliberately cut through the foundation trench after the wall had been removed. Perhaps this deposit was an offering of thanks or a 'goodbye' and it is difficult to resist the idea that this deliberate ritual marked the end of the settlement. The land it occupied was soon re-enclosed as fields, and cultivated again.

36 Headlands, West Overton, from the air looking east across the Saxon estate boundary, represented now by the sinuous hedge, between West Overton and East Overton. Nothing shows up clearly in the latter's root-crop, but in the cereal crop nearer the camera are many archaeological features showing up as crop-marks. They include, in the foreground, a rectilinear enclosure, possibly with internal structures; beyond it an echelon of three rectangles made up of individual dots, interpreted as timber structures perhaps of early medieval date; the semi-circle (the other half has been revealed on other air photographs) of a ditch around a late prehistoric settlement enclosure with an entrance to the left and many pits inside; ditches of a Roman settlement centre right; and a ditched rectangular enclosure, extreme centre right, possibly containing a small villa.

We shall not pursue the history of the site for we are chasing settlements here and this place was never lived on again. But it had certainly proved an interesting spot. The fact that we accidentally came across a burial place in excavating a much later settlement makes us wonder how many other flat cemeteries remain undiscovered under the grass. In the search for 'missing' settlements, our glimpse of the earliest round house, also found by accident, suggests that, despite the excellent archaeological preservation on the surface of these downs, much of the downland story lies beneath the grass in invisible, ancient landscapes. They were almost certainly much more crowded than we imagine, even for a well-explored area like this. After all, everywhere we excavated we found material earlier than the earthworks we were excavating and were able to establish a sequence of happenings on that spot, usually extending over many centuries into Roman and medieval times.

We now leave prehistory to explore those Roman and medieval periods as we continue to look for our dwellers on the downs.

6

Finding some farmsteads

The Romans found an empty downland prairie, so they ploughed it up. Suddenly the downs, where we saw evidence of prehistoric people everywhere but could only pin them down to their habitations with difficulty, were full of people, many of them living there. Settlements of the Roman era, identifiable by their characteristic pottery, appear on the downs in some number but what strikes us is their lop-sided distribution. Only two possible ones exist on Fyfield Down; whereas between the Roman road to the south and the northern end of Overton parish, at least six occupy Overton Down (**30**). If they were all occupied simultaneously, that makes quite a crowded landscape, particularly as much of the space between them was under cultivation. Quite a busy landscape, too, with people out in those fields much of the time, not forgetting the military supervisors ensuring that the development and use of this new landscape went according to plan. At a guess, then, in around AD 100, hundreds, perhaps even a thousand, people were living on these downs, the largest population they have ever witnessed.

The settlement areas were concentrated in two places in Overton. One was on the downland slopes overlooking the Kennet valley, east from Overton Hill. The other was further north on higher ground, but in a similar sloping, south-facing position just above the dry valley of Pickledean (**37**). We did no excavation at the first and there is virtually nothing to see on the ground as a result of cultivation lasting some 200 years. Fieldwork was, as ever, useful, despite so much land being under the plough. In addition, the National Monuments Record holds some splendid air photography of the area between Overton Hill and 'Headlands'. This last is the name we invented for the late prehistoric enclosed settlement crossed by the Anglo-Saxon boundary between East and West Overton (**36**). We gave it that name because the tenth-century land charter described this area as *heafde*, or 'headlands'.

We can separate out, at least as a working interpretation, the various elements making up the 'Headlands' settlement complex. The earliest is the settlement enclosure of *c*.700 BC, shown on air photographs to be packed with pits and exited by two gateways. Downhill, and stretching as far as the Roman road, a large Roman settlement is evidenced on the photographs by ditched enclosures and on the ground by bits of pottery. It may include a small villa in one of the enclosures, along with other dwellings, gardens, yards or animal paddocks. The villa crop-mark appears to show a typical Roman corridor building facing east, with short wings projecting east at both ends. The plan is familiar and credible, and perfectly acceptable to us; but others doubt the villa's existence at all, a nice example of the same evidence meaning different things to different people. For present purposes, we have a villa, one of only two in the land of Lettice Sweetapple. Is it just coincidence, we wonder, that each of our two parishes contains a Roman villa? Is it possible to think that the idea of a local territory or estate, much later to become enshrined in the medieval parish, might be as early as Roman times or even earlier?

Possibly relevant to that thought is a third and later phase in the settlement history, but one entirely dependent on air photographs and, again, controversial. We think we can

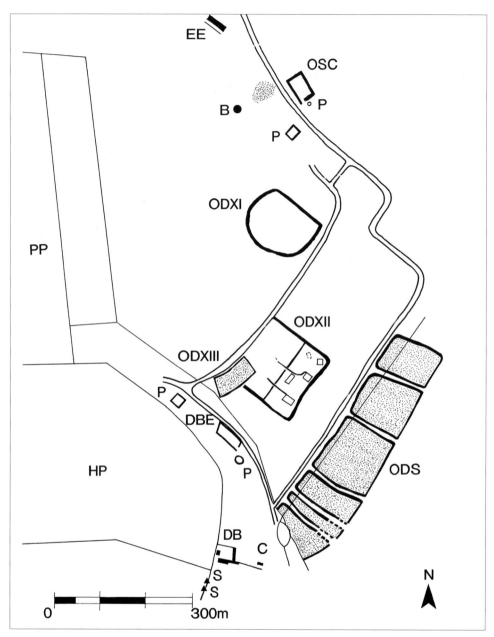

37 Map of the Down Barn area and northwards on to the southern half of Overton Down, showing schematically the main Roman or earlier tracks and the location of the main individual archaeological sites but not the context, notably field systems, in which they occur.

Key: *B Bronze Age round barrow; C Down Barn cottage; DB Down Barn; DBE Down Barn Enclosure; EE experimental earthwork; HP 'Hackpen Park'; ODXI later prehistoric settlement Overton Down site XI; ODXII late Roman settlement Overton Down site XII; ODXIII Roman settlement Overton Down site XIII; ODS Roman settlement Overton Down South; OSC rectangular earthwork enclosure interpreted as Overton sheepcote, with (stippled area on its west) the minimal area of an adjacent Romano-British settlement; P pond; PP Parson's Penning; S standing stone.*

*38 Excavation in progress, late Roman settlement, site Overton Down XII: the north east corner of the small mid-fourth-century building forming one of pair 'a' in **40**, showing the nature of the walls before any stones were removed by excavation, and the situation of the lower stone of a hand-mill on discovery (**colour plate 22**).*

discern three, possibly four, large timber buildings close to the prehistoric enclosure; and we like to think that they may be the headquarters buildings which succeeded the villa. Others cannot see them, or dispute their interpretation as buildings, so they cannot have the pleasure of theorising; whereas our only real doubt is whether they were built by the very last Britons in the later fifth–sixth centuries or some early Anglo-Saxons in the sixth or seventh centuries. Either way, we are fairly confident that the significant fact about this long-lived and apparently prestigious settlement over nearly a thousand years is that its history is played out on a boundary, a boundary which is still there today, and is a bridle way to boot.

Across the slope and on to Overton Hill were the north–south boundaries of what we think were Roman fields (chapter 4) and another settlement. It is a complex site of several phases, both pre- and post-Roman. A large, five-sided enclosure could well be Roman, perhaps occupied but perhaps simply a cattle or sheep enclosure. There is nothing else like it on the downs so we are entitled to think of it as special and linked perhaps either to the operations of our hypothetical Roman villa estate or to a continuing religious tradition on Overton Hill (and there are three remarkable Roman barrows between it and the ancient site of The Sanctuary). The site survived as impressive earthworks until about 1960, and its subsequent degradation by ploughing is well-recorded on air photographs. In fact one of them in 1924 was the first to record its existence, for this site had not previously appeared in the antiquarian literature or on maps; so, since it is nameless and was first recorded by O.G.S. Crawford, we have called it the 'Crawford complex' (**30**). Going round the countryside and giving names to 'new' old features is, as the reader may have gathered, one of the incidental pleasures of archaeological fieldwork.

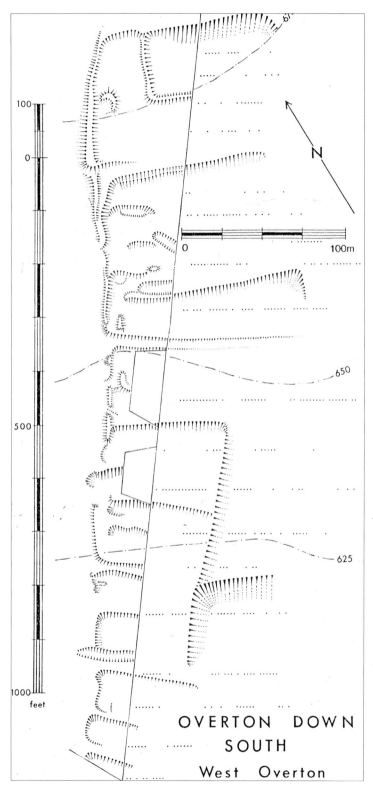

OVERTON DOWN
SOUTH

West Overton

39 Plan of the settlement called Overton Down South which lies directly opposite Down Barn, stretching for about ¼-mile (400m) up the south-facing slope. A narrow strip of the settlement survives remarkably well as earthworks against the extreme southern edge of the National Nature Reserve defined by a fence dividing old grassland from permanent arable. East of the fence, the remaining traces of the settlement are slight but it does not appear to have extended further than shown. This gives an overall impression of regularity to the site, especially with a repeating pattern of closes and tracks at intervals of c.70 yards (65m). It is certainly Roman, judging by surface finds, and apparently began early. It is interpreted as having been planted by the conquerors as part of their

The second focus of Roman settlement is less than two miles (3km) away to the north east. Here we did excavate, which, as usual, raised as many questions as it answered. On the ground opposite Down Barn lie three Roman settlements, crossed by two rights of way and all within the National Nature Reserve and Scheduled as Ancient Monuments — in other words, look and only take away pictures (**colour plate 19**)! The largest settlement is a series of rectangular enclosures (cottages with yards?) arranged symmetrically up and down the slope over nearly half a mile (800m). This settlement — let's call it a Roman village — once stretched eastwards, but that part has lain in arable for a thousand years and more. Potsherds from the modern plough-soil here suggest a date early in the Roman period for its occupation.

The smallest settlement (OD XIII) lies only some 300 yards (280m) to the west of the larger Roman village, in an area of very slight earthworks which we only saw convincingly in low evening light when the grass was very short in 1996. The humps and bumps suggest the former existence of perhaps three or four houses, again in rectangular enclosures; but there is no dating evidence other than that this site in 1996 looked very similar to the appearance of what we called Site ODXII in 1964. The third settlement is ODXII. It lies in between the other two settlements. Again, the slight earthworks here suggest buildings tucked into the corners of earlier fields (**40**). That is exactly what they turned out to be, for we excavated almost the whole site.

The history of these three settlements is not, however, as clear cut as the description above may imply. In fact they present a real puzzle: they are so close together that it is difficult to believe that they are not one and the same site. Indeed, the problem is worse, for there is a fourth settlement immediately to the south in Pickledean itself. This one is not visible on the surface and we only found it when excavating the banked and ditched Down Barn Enclosure on the floor of the dene. We thought it might be Roman but it was in fact later (how much later, we discuss later). The occupation material there is generally of first- or second-century AD date, so this site could be part of the Roman village only 200 yards (*c*.200m) away to the south-east.

It would be so convenient if we could lump all four sites together into one large and quite impressive early Roman town, planted on the downs as part of the reorganisation of the downland landscape in the first/second centuries AD. Unfortunately that won't work, for ODXII proved to be 'late', in fact in Roman terms very late, from about AD 340 until well into the fifth century. This, of course, opens up a whole new set of questions about who was living on the downs then, and why? And doing what, we might well add?

The ODXII settlement (**40**) was probably a farm, though its inhabitants were obviously not ploughing the fields on top of which it sat. Ploughing those particular fields had been abandoned at least 150 years previously after use during the early Roman landscape phase, presumably by those living in the Roman village a few yards to the south-east. The remains we excavated suggested we were dealing with one or two families, but possibly three for in our interpretation here we have added a putative house where we did not excavate in yard 'a'. In all we excavated five buildings: one certainly a milling shed ('a') (**38, colour plate 22**), one certainly a house forming a pair with an agricultural building (in yard 'b') (**colour plate 20**), and one probably a barn or byre (**colour plate 21**) but also lived in and forming another pair with an incompletely excavated, probable work-shed particularly associated with burning processes (in yard 'c').

All the buildings, except the 'burning building' in 'c', had started out as wholly timber structures. Later, however, each of them was remodelled. The timbers were dismantled and low stone walls were built in shallow foundation trenches to support a timber frame.

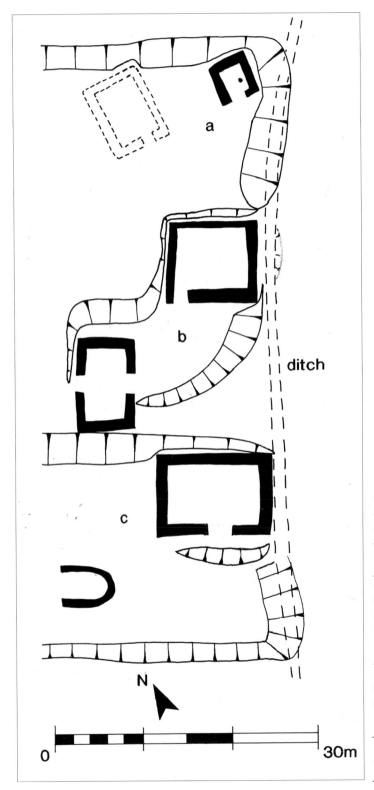

40 Plan of Overton Down XII, an excavated late Roman settlement, showing in solid black the outlines of the stone phases of the five buildings excavated, plus (dotted top left) another possible building required to support the particular interpretation here of three pairs of buildings, a-c. The whole, whether or not of three houses each with an ancillary building, was inserted into corners of fields cultivated in the first century AD; the settlement itself dates from mid-fourth/fifth century.

Woven wood (wattle) panels were then fitted into the frame on top of the stone walls. The wattle was then plastered with a mixture of clay, straw and animal dung (daub) or chalk, clay and straw (clunch): we found bits of daub but not clunch. All the buildings, except the apsidal-ended one in 'c' which was buried, were immediately under the turf and were marked by a stone or stones sticking through the grass.

Two interpretations present themselves for this Roman farm. Either it is one cottage in yard 'b' with a range of farm buildings round about, each with different functions but not necessarily all up and working at the same time; or — and this we favour — we are looking at three pairs of farms, each consisting of a building for habitation and one work-place. But you can see the trap coming that we have set ourselves: the small building with the hand-millstone still in place in yard 'a' then becomes the work-shed of the third pair, but where is the house? Well, we did not find it because at the time of excavation we did not look for it; but we would guess, having been back to look, that it lies immediately to the west, just outside the area we excavated.

Whatever the configuration, the dating is reasonably clear for, in addition to a large quantity of pottery, there were lots of late-Roman coins. A first phase, probably taking in the timber structures, was around the middle of the fourth century. The site then appears to have flourished, with the building of the stone-footed buildings, up to the late fourth century AD. There was then a third phase, some time in the first half of the fifth century, focusing on yard 'c'. The rest of the settlement might have been abandoned by then. There was a fourth phase too, a time when the whole site was very heavily robbed, in particular of its stone and other building material. This last phase came as a surprise, for we thought at first we were excavating an untouched site, meaning one not disturbed since the people walked out. This was not the case, however, for, as we soon came to realise, we were left not with the bits and pieces left by the occupants, but the bits and pieces left by the robbers. Such debris, we suppose, was either out of sight or not worth removing in the mid-fifth century — or later.

Some of these disregarded bits and pieces tell us a lot about our farm and its people as settlers in an already much-used landscape. There were constructional items, all broken and incomplete. These included one or two architectural fragments in non-local stone such as Cotswold limestone. There were baked clay floor tiles and *imbrices*, that is box flue tiles (though it is difficult to imagine that anyone here enjoyed central heating), and there were lots of bits of sandstone roof tiles from the north Somerset area. So, unless our late Roman downland Overtonians were assiduous collectors of rich men's debris, the hint (however uncomfortable the implications) is that our settlement was a few more notches up the social scale than that of a basic peasant farm. In fact, it may have been robbed of its building material precisely because it was worth taking. We also retrieved bits of broken bronze spoons and one complete toilet set, comprising an ear-scoop, tweezers and nail-cleaner still on their ring: definitely worth taking but presumably unseen by the looters. Again such things prompt the thought that 'well, if those things were left behind, what things of a similar class did the inhabitants possess that were taken away?'. And such removal could, after all, have been by the departing inhabitants as much by scavengers thereafter.

The pottery constituted a typical late Roman collection for the area, if anything a little drabber than most. Despite the usual imports from the potteries in the Oxford, Weald, New Forest and Poole Harbour areas, it was in no way special. Perhaps the most eloquent single pot, especially as it came from a 'late' context, was a complete flanged bowl of Roman form but non-industrial manufacture in a coarse clay with local grits. A good

41 Map of tithings, broad rig and sheepcotes on the downs. The four tithings are, from bottom left to right, West Overton, East Overton, Lockeridge and Fyfield, with some features in Clatford. The broad rig, or ridge and furrow, was plotted from air photographs quite independently of the tithing boundaries; the respect of the former for the latter, except across the Lockeridge/Fyfield boundary, was only observed later. Of the five sheepcotes shown (black squares), 1 is the Penning on West Overton Cowdown, certainly a post-medieval sheepcote; 2 represents an interpretation of the physically existing, post-Roman Down Barn Enclosure as the documented 'Hackpen' sheepcote; and 3 interprets the similar earthwork enclosure on Overton Down as the missing Overton sheepcote. All three sites are beside Roman settlements. The two known thirteenth-century settlement sites, Raddun and The Beeches on Manton Down (R and B), are shown as black circles; Raddun is interpreted as the documented sheepcote in this area (4) and The Beeches (5) site is guessed to be another.

collection of tools rather surprisingly left behind leaves no doubt of the agrarian and practical nature of the settlement. The two large chisels are particularly fine.

And then there is the glass, hundreds of fragments remarkable in three respects. While some bits come from bottles and jars, some of them are from tableware. These were fine things like glass cups and plates, implying formal meals and a lifestyle, or pretensions to one, that come somewhat unexpectedly from the context of late-Roman Overton Down. As a collection, the glass carries the date of occupation as late as it is possible to be in what was surely a rapidly diminishing 'Roman' Britain, that is well towards the middle of the fifth century. And thirdly, some of the fragments come from vessels which are not only very late but are rare and exotic. They come from what is now Belgium and the Rhineland, and have previously only been found in Britain in cities like Lincoln.

Our Site OD XII is, then, an enigma. It served the original purpose of our excavation in dating the underlying fields to the first two centuries AD, but then asked some other questions by dating itself to the fourth and fifth centuries, a period of great interest and ambiguity locally and not without a national dimension too. To be fair, here in some respects the evidence is unambiguous: it depicts a farmstead through the century or so of its life, changing a bit but essentially getting on with growing cereals, shepherding and preparing food and other products from them. But who were the people there and why were they there? — this is the ambiguous zone of interpretation. Here are two guesses, taking into account the exotic material and late date.

They were former workers, even slaves, on a villa estate, perhaps centred on the Headlands villa less than 2 miles (3km) to the south. Long before the formal end of Roman rule, we could suppose, the owners had left an increasingly disrupted countryside for good and now spent their time in the relative security of *Cunetio* (near Marlborough) and *Verlucio* (Sandy Lane near Calne), the nearest small towns, or perhaps even *Aquae Sulis* (Bath). The slaves they left behind thus enjoyed the freedom to farm what had become, in practice, their own lands on the margins of the estate. They set out their buildings on, literally, a green field site where they aped their former masters in using materials and domestic items brought from the villa site and kept as souvenirs of bygone days.

Alternatively, OD XII was inhabited by the estate owners and/or their professional staff, such as the estate manager. In this scenario they would have been forced to leave the villa itself, rather dangerously exposed as it was close to a main road along which gangs of threatening strangers, apparently landless, homeless and impecunious, were now tending to roam. At a time of an increasing break down of law and order, the villa-people opted for a familiar place to live on a south-facing slope but one hidden away in a fold in the downs. To it they took as much as they could of the materials from their former home. For a while they were successful in keeping up some semblance of a Roman lifestyle, though with increasing desperation as their supplies ceased to be available and they inevitably broke or lost their remaining Roman crocks, glass, tools and personal knick-knacks.

The final enigma is who robbed the site and where did they take their loot ? We just do not know. But the clear implication is that somewhere nearby a new, late-Roman building, possibly a farmstead, with stone foundations was built in the second half of the fifth century AD. There is scant evidence of people living permanently on the downs between the end of the fifth century (the end of OD XII) and AD 1200. A few people were buried in the traditionally sacred turf of the Bronze Age barrows on — need we name it? —Overton Hill in the fifth and sixth centuries. It is intriguing to think they might have lived nearby, since they seem to be Saxons rather than Britons and therefore represent some of the earliest Saxon people in the area. Perhaps their kinsfolk, not yet saved by Christian missionaries,

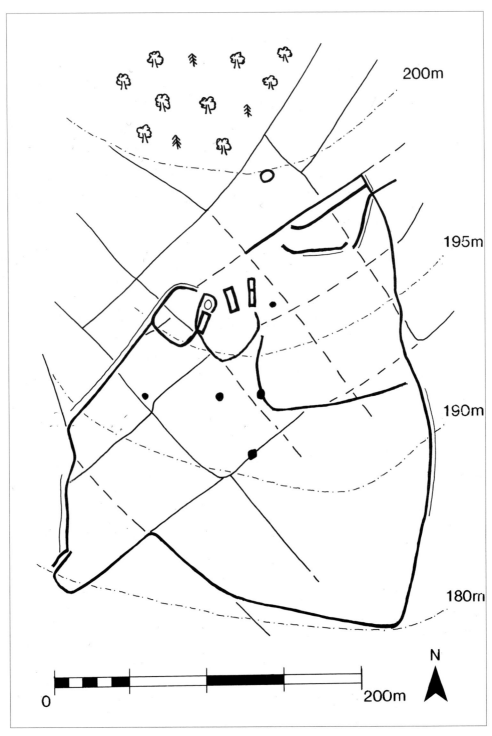

42 *Plan of Wroughton Mead with Raddun medieval settlement. The whole layout of the medieval complex (heavy lines) is conditioned by that of the pre-existing field system (thin lines), here partly restored (broken thin lines) from what is visible on the ground.*

*43 Late thirteenth-century farmhouse (Building 1, **44**), Raddun, Fyfield Down, viewed from the northern, uphill end. The walls were subsequently excavated fully and the baulks removed, but the main features are already clear. The nearer end, as far as the central ranging pole, was originally a house with opposed doorways and alcoves to either side, built in the second half of the thirteenth century. An extension was then added, on a slightly different alignment as the line of three post-footings marked by ranging poles indicates, with a new, wider doorway being provided facing east at the junction of the buildings. This 60ft (19m) long building was abandoned within a year or two of AD 1317. Beyond it is Rodden Mead with sheep to the left, and the Valley of Stones dropping to Clatford Bottom top left; on the central skyline is Martinsell Hill beyond West Woods.*

were the first to call Lockeridge Dene 'Woden's Dene' and Hursley 'the place where the horses are worshipped'.

Between that time and our next certain farmstead, our Anglo-Saxon charters depict a busy downland landscape. On the whole the downs were grazed and ploughed, yet somewhere a tenth-century cattle farm waits to be discovered. The charter for East Overton, in an odd attachment, refers to the *'feoh wicuna'*, a cattle farm set apart from the main estate. As we are fairly sure we have correctly mapped this Saxon boundary, the dairy farm appears to lie on Overton Cow Down, now called Fyfield Down, not far from Wroughton Copse. So when we find a man called Richard living at Wroughton Mead in 1248, or Raddun, the 'red down', as it was then known, of course we want to know who he is, why he is there and what he is doing.

His farmstead, though he did not know it at the time, was the one PJF visited on his first walk over Fyfield Down (see Chapter 3). Archaeologically the site consisted of two small, linked enclosures within a much larger enclosed area (**44**). Sir Richard Colt Hoare, Wiltshire's master local historian and pioneer landscape archaeologist, rode up to it one morning about 1818, perhaps exactly 500 years after its desertion. He caused an excavation to be made:

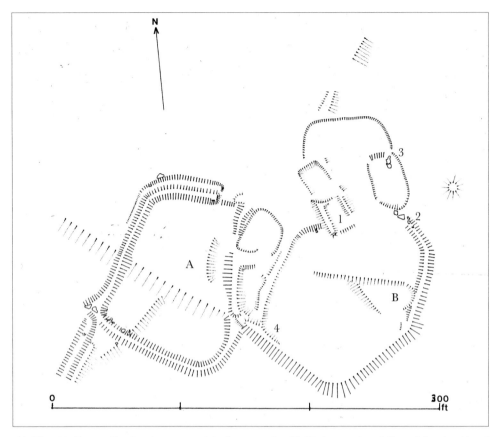

44 Plan: Raddun medieval settlement as originally surveyed, with Enclosures A and B overlying the sides of prehistoric fields, and Buildings 1–4. Building 4 is interpreted as that of Richard in 1248, by which time the site had changed from a sheepcote, with a timber building under Building 2, to a farmstead with a long-house.

Steering my course [from Devil's Den] westward towards Abury, I ascended the hill to a piece of down designated in the Wiltshire map by the name of Rowden Mead, upon which we again meet the undoubted vestiges of an extensive British settlement. On digging into one of the many excavations, the first stroke of our pick-axe brought up one half of a quern, or hand mill-stone, with its perforation in the centre, the tip of a deer's horn, and various fragments both of British and Roman pottery.

Again, although he did not realise it, Hoare had casually carried out what must have been one of the very first excavations of a medieval downland settlement. At the end of the twentieth century, our somewhat less casual excavations of the 1960s remain one of the few such in Wessex. We see reflected here the long antiquarian tradition that the downs belong to prehistory, to the Ancient Britons, with a bit of interference from Romano-Britons later. Certainly, in the infancy of medieval archaeology, people wondered why on earth we persisted in excavating near Wroughton Copse in the 1960s once we knew it was medieval, when so much of earlier date, by implication much more interesting, lay around us on the downs of the Avebury area. But we thought Richard was interesting in himself and he clearly represented a hitherto unexplored phase in the history of the downland landscape.

Excavation showed the settlement to contain six buildings, one of the sixteenth century, the other five of the thirteenth and early fourteenth centuries. Five buildings to the farmstead over about 100 years: that sounds familiar. It is of course of the same order in number and time as was the case on the two Overton Down farms (OD XI around 700 BC and OD XII around AD 400). This seems unlikely to be coincidence. It reflects the basics that a single family farm requires at any one time: a house and one or more ancillary buildings. In addition, looking at our evidence in these downland circumstances (with a more or less similar climate over the last three millennia), a neat theory is that Nature dictates that a farm — homestead and land — is sustainable only for about a century, for about three or four generations. Raddon conforms to that proposition (**43–5, colour plate 23**).

The farmstead we excavated began life as a sheepcote in about 1220. Yet tantalisingly four sherds of seventh/eighth-century pottery were found at Raddon, so perhaps we have here the cattle farm mentioned in the East Overton Saxon charter. At first, then, Raddon was probably just a shelter for the cattle, sheep and herdsman. It must have remained a good place to handle animals and to live, for in 1248 Richard was in residence at Raddun. He was there by special permission of the lord of the manor. This lord, as so often in the history of this landscape, was a distant and remote person, the Prior of St Swithun's at Winchester, himself beholden to the Bishop. Remote in distance and in person, maybe, but not bureaucratically. The medieval estates of the Bishop of Winchester were among the largest, richest and most efficient in the realm, and Richard was at the sharp end of a direct line of management accountability, as we would now put it. No rural idyll his, therefore.

45 Excavated medieval oven, Raddun, viewed from the east. The internal packing has been removed to expose the foundations of a structure of which the floor would have been at the level of the large stones on the rim of its external wall, surmounted by some sort of dome structure. The oven is of the type in which a fire was lit to heat the internal stones and then raked out before the material to be heated was inserted. Probably for drying grain as well as baking, it was built around AD 1300 into the northern end of the first house of the farmstead, here to the left (Building 4), and over the edge of a large earlier pit, here seen dropping past the right-hand ranging pole (scales in feet).

46a Wroughton Copse and Delling Enclosure, Fyfield Down, viewed looking east from Overton Down on the hollow-ways of the Marlborough-Avebury 'Green Street'. Wroughton Copse, left centre, is a distinctive landmark in this downland landscape; Raddun medieval farmstead is immediately to the right of its right hand corner, behind the hedge. Left centre is the outline of the rectangular Delling Enclosure, another farmstead and probably, in some sense, Raddun's successor in the sixteenth century. The Enclosure can probably be identified with the 'Dyllinge' of the 1567 Pembroke Survey.

46b Wick Down Farm Enclosure, Rockley, probably the site of the Templars' chapel in the thirteenth century. The earthwork enclosure clearly overlies part of extensive medieval settlement remains around the Farm.

47 The main London-Bath road across the downs offered a short-cut between Marlborough and Avebury, avoiding the winding way through the villages on the Kennet's south bank in medieval times and the toll-charging turnpike along the north bank from the eighteenth century. Locally now called 'Green Street', it is still called 'Herepath' by the Ordnance Survey. It is not 'Herepath', which is the Anglo-Saxon name for what we now call the Ridgeway. Officially closed to through-traffic in 1815-16 at Enclosure, the road is here passing between the Delling Enclosure, to the left, and Delling Cottage to the right, heading west off Fyfield Down, across the dry and here largely cleared Valley of Stones, and up the eastern slope of Overton Down. The great fan of holloways to the left is mirrored in Delling Wood to the right, indicating how wheeled traffic literally went out of its way to avoid already rutted tracks, and could do so on unenclosed downland. It also indicates how such traffic struggled to climb the slope and slithered and slid with its brakes locked to descend it.

As tenant he had to look after the manorial oxen, ensure the land was properly ploughed, provide two dozen eggs at Easter and keep the downs safe from attacks by wolves and thieves (his full brief is printed in chapter 10). He worked to the reeve who had to produce accounts for the Prior, often accompanying them with variously convincing explanations as to why targets had not been met. It all sounds terribly familiar.

The beauty of all this from our point of view is that the records of this system were made and kept centrally, and they have survived in the Cathedral archive. So in the summer of 1995, one of our team was able to go there and physically manhandle the custumals of the second half of the thirteenth century. These great rolls of vellum, that is animal hide, contain, in among masses of other annual accounts, the details of how Richard of Raddun had performed as a tenant. These records also contain some details of expenditure of the sort that St Swithun's as landlord, rather grudgingly one senses, had incurred. Thus we know that in 1309 the sheep were treated for *murrain*, an ovine disease, and a roof was repaired after that winter's terrible storm.

But, as must be expected, such splendid and illuminating documents seldom tell us all sorts of things we would like to know, for example what they ate or what they did when not engaged in the lord's work. But we have to remember that the documents were produced by a narrowly focused bureaucracy for one reason only, management information at the time, not for our delectation now. So, documents give us the tenurial situation and something of the economic history of the settlement, but it is the archaeology which tells us most about the different buildings and their histories, as well as the structural and gastronomic history of the whole site.

We found that the house that Richard had built and lived in was a stone-footed 'long-house', that is a rectangular building with a single, central doorway. Through it animals, here the oxen of the plough-team, entered and turned left. Richard and his family entered and turned right. So man and beast lived together under the same roof. The cattle were on the downhill side, where the byre had a central drain which emptied under the downhill gable wall to an outside pit. Naturally, all manure was keenly collected. In the other half, human comfort of a sort was derived from the warmth of the cattle in the next room and a hearth against the northern wall. Just up from the only door was the rubbish pit and across the yard lay the sheep-house (**44**, Buildings 4 and 2).

In the 1270s or 1280s, with Richard now dead, the farm expanded and was improved, perhaps by Richard's son but the documents do not name the tenant now. A new house was built a little to the east, leaving Richard's long-house to the elements. The new farmhouse was surely the latest in design in its day. Gone were the old, unpleasant arrangement of Man and beast under one roof. Though the house retained the two room room plan, a solid wood partition now divided the living quarters from a barn and the animals were moved to a sheep-cote and stable across a cobbled yard (**colour plate 23**). Some smithying took place, perhaps not only to shoe the horses and oxen, but also to cater for the travellers following the high downland tracks (**47**). A good, well-built oven (**45**) was set into the ruins of Richard's house and new enclosures around the farm were also added (**42**). Chickens, horses, pigs, goats, cows and sheep were kept, as were sheep-dogs. Vegetables and fruit were no doubt grown near the farm and geese, ducks, game birds and deer were hunted. There was also a fairly large area of open field laid out in strips to the east, and villagers came up the mile or so (1.6km) from the valley to tend them. Clearly the monks had decided to invest on a large-scale in the economy of East Overton. Soon, the manor became one of the largest and most prosperous estates on their books.

So Raddun flourished. Its fall came quite quickly and probably unexpectedly. It was thriving throughout the latter years of the 1200s and the early years of the fourteenth century. By 1318, however, it was deserted. Its inhabitants simply walked out (see Chapter 10). They took their family heirlooms in the safe-box which had been hidden under the wall of the barn, or at least most of its contents, and walked down to the valley.

7

Visiting the villages

Anyone walking into the valley in the early fourteenth century would have found a long-settled landscape. We too would recognise it, for it was not very different from what we see today. There would have been more trees, especially elms, and the River Kennet, more convincingly a river but more sluggish than now, wound its way between willows and reeds except where it had been canalised to drive manorial mills, now long-gone. The basic structure of today's landscape, however, was not only already there round about AD 1300, it was already at least 700 years old.

The four villages of Saxon times, Fyfield, Lockeridge, and East and West Overton, were still there in 1318 and, give or take bits and pieces and a hundred yards here and there, were situated basically where they are now along the river valley. All the villages look different now, however, for they have all altered their appearance quite dramatically over the last thirty years, and we know of similar changes in the later and earlier nineteenth century from cartographic evidence. Earlier, a conversion in building methods from timber-framed to stone-walled houses would have created a similar visual effect. A picture of both continuity and change begins to emerge.

Modern local studies have produced a similar picture over much of Britain. Yet there remains a common belief that the English village represents only antiquity, permanence and stability. Something psychological seems to lurk here, as if we need re-assurance that 'some things never change'. Advertisers like it that way too, forever churning out the clichés showing smiling, servile peasants crafting in pretty olde-tyme village streets down which happy, bygone horses clip-clop but never defecate. Somehow we do not think life was quite like that in our real-time medieval villages, but such images are useful. They recognise that change has in fact happened, the implication being that we have lost the unchanging rural idyll of supposedly healthy village life. The historical truth is, of course, that villages before the mid-twentieth century were among the least suitable places around which to image concepts of a healthy or unchanging past.

Many villages are nevertheless a thousand years or more old. They are, however, characteristically a relatively late arrival in an English countryside already fashioned and formed, as we have seen, by people living in other places during the preceding millennia. Nor are they as a type of settlement permanent fixtures in the medieval landscape. Many, for example, had been founded and deserted long before the Norman Conquest, and thereafter several thousand failed the test of permanence up to our own day in the face of economic flux, environmental change, plague and landlords' whim. And as for being stable! — taking a thousand-year view, villages have hopped around the landscape like fleas on a hedgehog and have changed in shape and size, merging and splitting, rather like amoebae slithering around on a glass slide beneath a microscope. Fyfield is a good example. Our villages exhibit all these characteristics. They are always there, from no later than AD 900 and in one case from about AD 100; but then you look again and one has disappeared completely; two have become one; and between and around all of

48 The Withy Bed, East Overton, a small area beside the manorial boundary on the valley floor at the bottom of Frog Lane which is now undrained and unkempt with a dense willow foliage. It is perhaps suggestive of prehistoric conditions though is actually an abandoned part of the man-made landscape. The later nineteenth-century tower of St Michael's church to the south east picks out the low knoll on which the original East Overton probably developed.

them smaller settlements — farms and hamlets — have come and gone. The landscape of settlement is not like a jigsaw in which all you have to do is find the right piece to fit and, hey presto! you can 'complete the picture'. It is much more like the image in a kaleidoscope: look and discern the patterns; tap it, marvel at the sight — and start again.

But none of these metaphors contains one of the vital ingredients which, in real life, often affords significant clues in trying to understand how the landscape 'worked'. We refer to words, and hence documentary evidence. All four of our main villages were documented in Domesday Book. What this means is that some time in 1086 account had to be rendered to the officials and scribes of William the Conqueror, accompanied by a translator, about the estates of the Kennet valley. The brief of the King's men was to record the size and value of the land, as well as the resources or major buildings attached to each estate, such as woodland, meadow, mills or fish ponds. This information was collected, not of course as historical evidence for us, but so that the Norman king could assess the taxable worth of his newly acquired realm.

Both before and after 1086, outstandingly useful to us were names, especially place-names and field-names, for after all what we were after was happening in the fields and woods as well as in the settlements. Both sorts of names came to play a major role in our enquiries. At one level the names of individual fields, even of single strips within an open field, came to be important, in identifying a specific archaeological site, for example; at another was the fairly basic matter of the name of our largest village. Two Overtons are 'hidden' beneath the single modern name 'West Overton'. Put another way, the 'West Overton' where Lettice lived 200 years ago was and was not the 'West Overton' of today's maps. This is but one of the several puzzles about where people lived along the valley which took us some time to crack.

Let us briefly visit each village in turn, travelling from west to east: West Overton, East Overton, Lockeridge and finally Fyfield. Two of the main points to emerge from our explorations are: that in this sample of 'ordinary' English villages, each is different from the others; and that the only historical experience that they all share is one of continual change.

THE OVERTONS

Local people will be surprised to see that sub-heading. 'Overtons' plural? Surely there is only one Overton, West Overton? The story goes something like this.

The existing village is wrongly called West Overton. It was created, at least in name, only a century ago, though its physical presence goes back a thousand years earlier. Today's village is actually made up of two villages, each belonging to a separate estate, each with its own history. The estate of Saxon West Overton belonged to the Abbess of Wilton and passed to the Earl of Pembroke at the Dissolution. Its main village was first of all right on the western edge of the estate, along what is now the Ridgeway by East Kennet. Some cottages are strung along the road there today but effectively this original West Overton, with its church (Chapter 9), might have already been abandoned by AD 972. Two tenth-century land charters clearly imply that 'old' West Overton had already moved by that date.

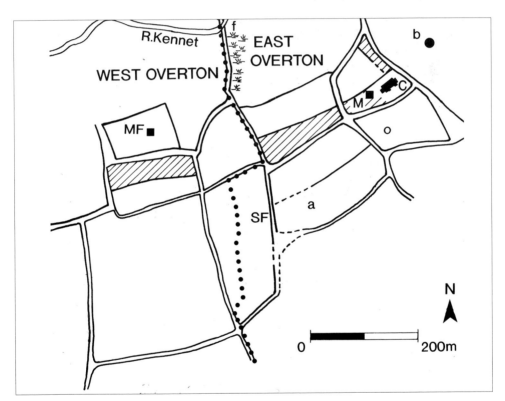

49 Plan of West and East Overton villages, schematically reconstituted as they probably were in the tenth century AD from the evidence of two Saxon charters, later maps and surviving elements in the villages' fabric. Much, but by no means all, of the road pattern shown still exists. This West Overton village, the second one, has no church, but a manor house and farm in one; East Overton had a manor house next to the church, with a separate farm at the other end of the village.

Key: Hatched areas: those parts of the Saxon villages still occupied today Dotted line: the tenth century estate boundary between the two Overtons, described in both AD 939 and 972 a that part of East Overton village now deserted and characterised by earthworks b Bronze Age round barrow C the Church of St Michael's and All Angels f ford via Withy Bed and Frog Lane M manor house MF manor house and farm o area, with earthworks, of possible original settlement of the 'Upper tun' SF South Farm.

50 The former East Overton with its church, now in the civil parish of West Overton. The view is from South Farm north-eastwards across horse paddocks containing the well-preserved earthworks of medieval settlement remains, now a Scheduled Ancient Monument. The trees and buildings to the left mark what remains of the medieval village along its main street leading up the gentle slope to the slight knoll where the settlement probably began (49).

A new West Overton was created over to the east. The village moved across the Abbess' estate to where it was to stay right up to the present day. It was put down beside the already existing East Overton, in effect making up the western half of a double village, the village now so misleadingly called West Overton. For that present village was clearly divided into two named settlements throughout medieval times. The western part was West Overton; the eastern part was East Overton. Each belonged to a separate manor. They were divided by the old estate boundary; the same point can be expressed by saying that each was built up against the old boundary. All this smacks very much of landlords' jostling for position and status.

Perhaps as much as eight centuries later, Lettice Sweetapple lived in this 'new' West Overton. Unfortunately, we do not know for certain when it was created. However, disguised among its streets, lanes and modern housing estates are the lineaments of a rectangular-shaped settlement. This included the manor farm at its north-west corner. The manorial mill, possibly on the same site as that referred to in the Domesday Book, was astride a leat immediately to the north. We suspect that the new village with its manorial fittings may have been laid out on hitherto arable land during a phase of ecclesiastical and land reform in the mid/late tenth century. It is just possible, on one reading anyway, that the AD 972 charter is telling us precisely that but, whether new or not, by that date the village of the West Overton estate was where it is now, occupying the land west of Frog Lane.

There was also Saxon East Overton (**48**). This today forms the eastern half of the village called West Overton, that is the area east of Frog Lane but including South Farm. This area contains the church, St Michael's and All Angels, but much of it is now a grass field between the church and the site of South Farm, destroyed in the 1960s. This apparently empty field, called Ring Close in 1819, is full of archaeological features — banks, lines of sarsens, house-sites and former lanes. Our survey sorted out the confusion, showing a recognisable pattern of abandoned settlement remains, in some sense presumably 'old' East Overton. Quite when 'old' was we do not yet know, for the field was virtually empty when it is first depicted on maps in the later eighteenth century (**50**).

Our best guess — and it really is no more — is that somewhere within the complex of earthworks, probably up near the church, is the earliest East Overton, Roman or Saxon up to about AD 900. We guess too that the earthworks themselves include, in what appears to be a distinctly rectilinear pattern of the sort that major landlords promoted, an element of planning which is broadly medieval and possibly late Saxon. Overall, together with South Farm and the houses still along the north side of the road up to the former manor house (**colour plate 24**) and church, we envisage this as representing medieval East Overton in, say, the thirteenth century. Desertion could have occurred for any one or more reasons thereafter, but we would hazard a guess for which there is no evidence at all — yet. Perhaps the site was simply cleared, of peasants, buildings and smells, in the later sixteenth century to improve the setting of, and view from, the much-improved medieval manor house, now becoming a gentleman's residence as a secular landscape began to emerge from the many tenurial changes following the Dissolution.

East Overton was always the more important Overton. It belonged to the Bishop of Winchester and was therefore part of, indeed a significant part of, one of the largest, richest and most powerful estates in England. So too was Fyfield, and the two manors tended to be run together, always with East Overton as the dominant partner. Indeed, East Overton was one of the pre-eminent Winchester manors, its 2256 sheep in 1248 representing a remarkable rate of growth in the thirteenth century. Yet East Overton has been almost forgotten and its former residents must be turning in their graves around St Michael's at the fact that the lesser, upstart West Overton has now blanketed their former existence by taking over the name of the village to which it was in fact an addition.

In 1086, of course, the distinction was quite clear to local people, and even the Domesday commissioners were in no doubt that two different places existed. Of Norman West Overton, they recorded that the manorial holding, or demesne, covered seven hides and was worked by two serfs with two ploughs. The rest of the villagers consisted of 11 peasants who farmed the remaining land, again with two ploughs. The Domesday entry also tells us that the estate contained five acres of meadow, 20 acres of pasture and eight acres of woodland, as well as a mill on the Kennet which paid 10s a year to the manor as rent.

Yet these early civil servants did not in fact complete their job and, as a result, we do not know how many people farmed the neighbouring estate of East Overton. Though the scribe left a space on the page, no-one returned to insert the information. King William may not have noticed, but we are sorely handicapped by that clerical oversight. We do know, though, that the land was worked by seven ploughs. So we can make a little calculation. If West Overton had 13 peasants working four ploughs, then with seven ploughs and assuming comparability between the manors, the adult males of East Overton could well have numbered around 20–25. This is a fair size for the late eleventh century. The village population could, therefore, have been well over a hundred on these hard figures alone, never mind our trying to estimate the number of people who, for whatever reason, did not enjoy the privilege of working the manorial ploughs.

East Overton also contained 15 acres (6ha) of meadow, a pasture eight furlongs long by four broad (about 320 acres; 130ha) and woodland five furlongs long by two broad (100 acres; 40ha). This large, rectangular area of pasture lay on the downs to the north of Down Barn, the southern part of Overton Down which had been so active in Roman times (see Chapter 6). We know from our study of the Saxon charters that this same area had been pasture for at least the 150 years before Domesday. It was more surprising to discover, however, that the woodland, described as a rectangular area of about 100 acres (40ha) in this 900-year-old document, reflects the size and shape of East Overton's wood throughout history, right up until the Second World War. We note later from other evidence in Chapter 8 that the location and extent of West Woods as a whole seem to have been stable since prehistoric times.

LOCKERIDGE

Lockeridge looks in many ways the least interesting of our villages. It has no church for picturesque cottages to cluster around, it is rather strung out and apparently formless, and much of it seems to be of rather unattractive Victorian and modern build. Yet in some ways it is the most unusual of the villages, and we have probably found out more that is new about it than the other villages simply by giving it due attention where others have passed it by.

We shall touch on its Neolithic past and its long barrows in chapter 8. A Bronze Age burial turned up behind the school last century, and recent air photography has brought to light crop-marks of Bronze Age round barrows on White Hill, a ridge above the village. It has also produced marks of rectangular ditched enclosures there, perhaps indicating a farm of Roman date of which the banks and ditches may well have survived into the eighteenth century. This last evidence only came to light in 1995, reminding us that nearly sixty years previously the authors of Wiltshire's volume of place-names observed of the name 'Lockeridge' that it was conceivably derived from the Old English composite word *loc(a)-hrycg*, 'a ridge marked by enclosure(s)' (**colour plate 25**).

Nevertheless, all this is fairly routine stuff, with nothing except its name specific to the village as a village. Even the Domesday entry is at first sight not particularly unusual. *Locherige* was held in 1086 by Durand of Gloucester, the sheriff. Then it was just a 2-hide estate worth 30s. Half of it was in demesne, with the other half farmed by four peasants. It contained 6 acres of wood and only one of meadow. But Durand also held another 2-hide estate, attached to the Bishop of Winchester's East Overton manor - a minor holding but one which was to feature very significantly in our exploration of this landscape and its people as we tried to unpick the documentary complexities of Lockeridge's history (Chapter 10, St Quyntin). It was in the mid-twelfth century that Lockeridge became a bit different, but before indulging in that excitement let us just pause to look at pre-Norman Lockeridge.

To do this we need to look at the present village and maps of it going back to the eighteenth century. Beyond its north end, just across the river but still in the tithing, is Lockeridge House; and similarly just beyond its southern end is Lockeridge Dene, now a somewhat irregular collection of houses, including Lockeridge Dene House, around a triangular space and a dene-bottom still filled with sarsen stones. We suggest that these are the sites of two late-Saxon settlements going with the two estates identified for us by Domesday Book.

At the northern one are (and were) slight settlement earthworks. They lie across the present

51 Lockeridge House, built in the early eighteenth century (with later additions) but probably perpetuating a much older settlement of Lockeridge at a river crossing. This is the north front, with its lovely pineapple gateway, facing towards Fyfield and away from present-day Lockeridge village, across the Kennet to the south.

road from Lockeridge House (**51**) and over a field called 'Piper's Croft' towards the Roman road, here called 'Piper's Lane' in 1819. The name 'Piper' is intriguing: again rare, it is perhaps ascribing magical origins to something, a constructed road, which, like 'Devils Den', must have been mysterious to uneducated minds throughout a thousand years. In folklore, pipers, like fiddlers, are usually people petrified for doing something naughty but goodness knows what the offence was here. It seems likely that the relative eighteenth-century grandeur of Lockeridge House perpetuates habitation of a much older site occupying the land between the Roman 'Pipers' and the River Kennet. We do not know its name, though it may have been 'Lockeridge' in Anglo-Saxon times, even until the mid-twelfth century, perhaps because what we now call Lockeridge was not there: it is so simple when you think sideways!

At the other end of present-day Lockeridge is Lockeridge Dene. We propose that this is the settlement area for the other two-hide Domesday estate held, if we are right, by the person who was both Durand of Dene and Sheriff of Gloucester. It makes sense: much of the area used to be in East Overton manor and by the sarsens is a meeting place of two main routes. One comes off the downs from the north past Fyfield, the other comes along the Kennet valley from the east. Conjoined, they move south-west over Boreham Down and then through the main street of Shaw to the Vale of Pewsey below (Chapter 8; **55**). In other words, Dene was on a major communication way. It could even be that the small settlement itself was arranged in a triangle around an open space, a green, formed by the tracks' junction and a continuation of the local east-west road linking the villages along the south side of the Kennet. There was no through road in medieval times along the north side of the river unless you went over the downs from Marlborough to Avebury (**47**).

Our exploration of Lockeridge leads us to suggest that a brand-new village was laid out and built on the flat ground between these two Saxon settlements in the middle of the twelfth century. The occasion was the creation of an estate for and by the Order of the Temple, or Knights Templar. Between 1141 and 1143, the Order acquired one of the two-hide Lockeridge estates, we suggest that based on Lockeridge House. In 1155–6, it acquired land up on the downs at Rockley where it built its preceptory (**46b**). With another grant about the same time, by the end of the twelfth century the Templars were established with a remote place of worship and a three-hide estate called *Lokeruga* to support it and their community (Chapter 10).

Maps of Lockeridge up until the recent past show it as outlined by, and within, a compact rectangle of properties lying north-south from the former Gospel Hall to the former 'Masons Arms'. Such physical evidence strongly suggests that it has been laid out as a planned village at some stage, and it is difficult to resist the temptation to see the second half of the twelfth century as the time in question. A fairly compelling piece of new evidence came up — literally — after we had worked out that interpretation. Again the dry summer of 1995, again air photography, and this time the parch-mark of quite a large ditch lying along the east side of Lockeridge, as if the former boundary of the village was laid out parallel to the village street.

So we see dull looking Lockeridge village as being something quite rare in England, essentially a planned Templar village of the mid-to-late twelfth century. There is more to it than that for, as we have seen, this new village replaced and occupied some of the space between two earlier 'Lockeridges' half a mile (800m) apart (**55**). There are also two other stories to be told about this undistinguished place: its medieval settlements, including the mystery of Upper Lockeridge, and the Victorian village when … Well, they will have to wait for another day. But we must add something you might never think of: unlike Overton and Fyfield villages, modern Lockeridge has a pub — the 'Who'd a' Thought It'.

FYFIELD

Conventionally, the history of this small and very insignificant village ought to begin — and perhaps end — with Domesday Book. It was recorded as *Fifhide*, an estate name indicating that it was of five hides. It belonged to the Sacrist, or treasurer, of the Abbey at Winchester. A sole peasant farmed the three hides in demesne, though he did have two ploughs, while elsewhere on the estate 12 peasants farmed the remaining land, yet they too had two ploughs. Along the riverbanks, Fyfield had three acres of meadow, and sheep and cattle grazed 30 acres of land on the slopes north and south of the settlement. That's about it really; totally unremarkable (**52**).

We can, however, squeeze one quite significant observation out of these basic Domesday figures. Adding Fyfield's contribution to those of West Overton and Lockeridge, we can count 32 recorded farmers in our four villages. The number would more likely have been nearer 50 if the record of East Overton had been completed. It is possible the same number of other people has gone unrecorded. So, assuming our area contained between 50–100 heads of households and an average of ten people to the household, the population of Fyfield and Overton could have been between 500 and 1000 at the end of the eleventh century. This number, on the whole, probably reflects the population of our area through the twelfth and thirteenth centuries as well, right up until the arrival of the Black Death in 1348. Such numbers would have created quite a busy landscape; equally, that same landscape, well-farmed within the technological limitations of the time, could easily have sustained such numbers.

52 *Fyfield village, viewed from in front of Lockeridge House, showing the medieval church surrounded by an architecturally undistinguished huddle of buildings, backed by Fyfield Hill on the north side of the Kennet valley. The thin line of scattered stones across the centre of the photograph mark the line of the former Roman road, 'Piper's Lane', destroyed c.1970.*

Sir Richard Colt Hoare provides the vital clue that there may be more than meets the eye at Fyfield itself. Part II (1821) of his *Ancient History of Wiltshire* includes both our two parishes. Sir Richard recorded, without giving any source, that 'a rude Roman pavement was found on the property of Mr Tanner, immediately on the right of the turnpike at Fyfield'. Mr Tanner had lived in Manor Farm. This Farm was replaced by what is now called Fyfield House, a neo-classical country house called 'Mr Goodmans Homestead' on a map of 1819. We suspect that it was new at that time.

This would fit with its architectural style and with the social change proceeding along the Kennet valley. Newly well-off and self-important 'big' farmers, tenants and land-owners who were benefiting from Enclosure, built the sort of detached 'homesteads' they thought appropriate to their recently-acquired status (**colour plate 32**). In other words, the poorly constructed mosaic floor may well have come to light as Colt Hoare was collecting his material for his North Wiltshire volume in the years 1814-18, so he did not give a reference: he either saw the evidence or heard of it at first hand. That he was right cannot be doubted, for in recent years plentiful evidence of a substantial Roman establishment — probably a villa — has come to light along the river bank on the east side of the garden of Fyfield House. We wonder whether it was mere coincidence that brought to this same spot a villa, a manor house and a church. At the very least on this little bluff above the River Kennet, a thousand years witnessed some local concentration of wider authority, respectively to Rome, Winchester and Heaven, to Caesar, the Bishop and God.

53 St Nicholas' church, Fyfield, mainly flint with sarsen quoins, medieval but heavily restored in the nineteenth century. It stands close beside, possibly on, a Roman site that was probably a villa. Its box tombs by its south porch, partly visible here, are particularly fine, and Listed.

Fyfield village is the only place along the valley in our two parishes with clear evidence of Roman origins. Situated on the north bank of the river, it is one of only two villages so placed between Marlborough and Avebury. The other is West Kennet, astride the main London-Bath Roman road. As we have already seen on the northern downs, the imprint of ownership seems to have been clamped on the land early in the Roman period. Such authority may well have been exercised locally from a spot close to where Fyfield church and manor house later exercised their medieval power.

Fyfield is small, and always has been, its core always around where St Nicholas' church now stands (**53**). Paradoxically, however, remains of it as a settlement are extensive. This is because it has shuffled around over about half a square mile (*c*.800m x 800m) during the last two millennia. The main reason for this is almost certainly because its history is very much bound up with through-traffic, north-south as much as east-west and quadruped as much as wheeled. This may seem an odd conclusion about a place so insignificant that perhaps the only thing most motorists notice of it today is the road-sign announcing that they are entering 'FYFIELD', then whoosh!, it has gone. But probably it has always been a bit like that, for almost certainly it began as a road-side settlement.

In prehistoric and early historic times, it lay just to one side of a track descending from the Marlborough Downs to ford the Kennet en route for the Vale of Pewsey and, ultimately, the Channel coast. In Roman times, just over 300 yards (300m) south of the villa was the main road to Bath. The nearest Fyfield has to a village street, the narrow road south from the church, and then the footpath across the field towards Lockeridge, are probably on or close to the line of a side-road coming off that main road to the villa.

When the turnpike successor to the Roman road was built along the valley 1800 years later, just beyond the north side of the village, it pulled much of the village into a ribbon development along some 250 yards (250m) north-east of the church. That is where much of the village is shown when Fyfield first comes to appear on maps in Lettice's time, in the decades around AD 1800. It has moved twice more since then, but that is another story. We would add, nevertheless, that while we have been looking at it, Fyfield village has changed dramatically in appearance, entirely for the worse. Still, people doubtless complained when a brash new Roman villa, when a horribly clean-cut new stone church, when a startlingly fashionable new manor farm were built — they all changed the village's appearance. Now, in the form of new houses and aggressive land-use change, the later twentieth century has in turn left its mark on this local landscape.

8

Settling to the south

The landscape south of the villages is, like the villages themselves, both familiar and puzzling. Essentially, it has not changed much since Lettice's time, since medieval times and indeed since the Roman period. On the other hand, it contains at least as many queries and uncertainties as the downs to the north.

It is more varied in its shape, soils, vegetation and natural resources than the downs and, from the point of view of the landscape detective, has the great attraction that much less research attention has been paid to it than the 'scientifically sexy' downland. Forest is its dominant visual feature, though out of sight below the ground surface over the higher areas the presence of a relatively large spread of clay-with-flints over the chalk is influencing the history and appearance of this tract of countryside. It is the mix of woodland, open downland, sarsen stones and long, dry valleys, locally called denes, which give both interest and complexity to this landscape. It looks in a curious sort of way much more a natural countryside than the artifically created and maintained openness of downland. Its very appearance, however, is as managed as the 3000-year-old look of Overton and Fyfield Downs (**54**).

54 Landscape with trees and the hedges of enclosed fields south of Lockeridge, looking north across the Kennet valley towards Fyfield village over the house-tops in the middle distance. The lane climbs the slope from Lockeridge to the viewpoint, and then runs south to Breach Cottage and West Woods.

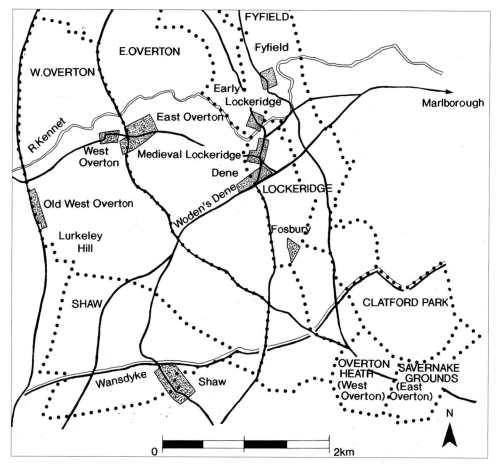

*55 Map of the medieval landscape of the valley and the woodland area (not delineated in the interests of clarity, see **56**), showing the boundaries of the five estates and some of the 'ancient' trackways through the area, the main settlements (stippled), six of which no longer exist as separate entities, and Clatford Park which was later incorporated into Fyfield to give the parish its modern shape. The heathland of the two Overtons was detached from the main manorial lands.*

Some of the earliest archaeological evidence in the study area comes from around what are the woodland edges now. They may well have been so as many as 7000 years ago too. People were around here then, on the south side of today's woods, using the plateau between the woodland and the steep drop into the Vale of Pewsey. The evidence comes not from archaeologists but from two Mr Bulls, father and son. They have been keeping their eyes open and collecting flints as they have farmed the fields of Bayardo Farm for over 50 years; and their eloquent collection, partly in Devizes Museum and supported by a good memory, is of Mesolithic and early Neolithic material from the millennia either side of 5000 BC. Much of it is of very good quality flint, used mainly for blades and scrapers of different types, shapes and sizes; but most of it is of waste material, that is the flakes and other debris produced in the making of tools. It is not difficult to imagine people who were primarily hunters coming up from their relatively sheltered habitation sites along the edges of the Vale of Pewsey to a well-known source of good flint — which we have yet to find — and staying awhile on the colder clay-with-flints plateau while they replenished their stock of tools and arrowheads. Doubtless they hunted too, in and around the edges of what much, much later was to become known as 'West Woods'.

That is about as prosaic a name you can find but, if you stop and think about it, is not something a little odd here? 'West' of what? The answer is 'Savernake Forest', formerly an extensive royal Forest but whose woodland is now confined to south and south east of Marlborough. But the woodland stretching across the southern zone of our area as far as the lands of Lettice in West Overton was, in medieval times, part of that Forest, at least in the sense that the royal writ ran over it to control hunting and other activities in it. So 'West Woods' were literally the woods in the western part of Savernake Forest.

We went to look at two known sites at the start of our exploration of this wooded landscape. One was in the south west of our study area, at a place called 'Shaw' (**55**). Again the name is an interesting one and, in southern England, quite rare. It derives from an early English word '*sceaga*', meaning 'small wood'. In West Yorkshire it seems often to have meant a wood on the edge of the main woodland area, which would exactly describe the position of Shaw Copse here — west even of 'West Woods'. Immediately west of that Copse was the site we had come to inspect, a deserted medieval village, but we found its northern part freshly ploughed. A rapid search of the plough-soil around the field's edges produced a small collection of the sort of rubbish found in the surface of most fields in England except that among it were flints like those collected on Bayardo Farm, and a few Neolithic potsherds. Not much in themselves, these bits and pieces nevertheless suggested early and long-lived activity in this unfashionable area in and around the forest.

A well-known early farming site lies nearby. Probably belonging to the fourth millennium BC, it is called Knap Hill; the structure is a hill-top enclosure with discontinuous ditch not far beyond the boundary of West Overton parish to the south-west (**colour plate 28**). Balancing Knap Hill topographically, as it were, just inside the far south eastern boundary of the parish, is a contemporary structure, a large, oval-shaped mound in West Woods. Covered by brambles, it supports a few beech trees and lies within the unimaginatively-named 'Barrow Copse' — with no hidden meanings in the name this time! This mound, some 120ft (37m) long, 14ft (4m) high and 66ft (20m) wide between two ditches, is an excellently preserved long barrow or burial mound. Partial excavation in somewhat surreptitious circumstances in 1880 apparently exposed a megalithic burial chamber containing 'black matter but no relics'. Just as well perhaps (**colour plate 26**).

These two sites hint that they may well be the visible fragments of a once-extensive Neolithic landscape hereabouts, now disappeared except for these two earthworks and, possibly, the edge of the woodland. We can suspect that, some 5000-5500 years ago, sufficient people were in the neighbourhood with enough of an investment in the land to think it worth their while to make a considerable communal effort to construct this useless-looking mound. Perhaps it was as much to their gods as for the burial of people, rather as parish churches were built and adorned some 3000 or more years later; and that its use extended to high-days and holidays as much as to Sun-days — the barrow is aligned west–east. In late twentieth-century jargon, its function was almost certainly to do with identity, bonding and social coherence as it was to dispose of the dead. Around it we can imagine people with flint tools and, later, stone axes, hunting birds and animals, camping and then settling, clearing trees and then farming, in and around the forested area of West Woods over the millennia up to about 3000 BC. People had been hunting there thousands of years before medieval kings and nobles.

This largely unstudied landscape was filling up before our eyes. Then 1995 produced some wonderful air photographic evidence as the long hot summer went on and on. Among it was the outline of a 'new' long barrow, showing as parch-marks on the hill above Lockeridge

1 *Overton Church, 1834: a watercolour showing the medieval church at the east end of East Overton village, 45 years before its transformation in 1879 into the existing parish church of St Michael and All Angels, West Overton.*

2 *The River Kennet flood-plain and treeless valley side, looking north from west of the village of West Overton across to the unenclosed northern part of the manor and the Ridgeway skyline beyond.*

3 Magnetometer survey, Wroughton Mead, with excavation of Raddun behind and Fyfield Down in the distance. The string mesh stretched out on the grass is to measure systematically changes in the earth's magnetic susceptibility and therefore, in this particular case, the presence or absence of further features of the medieval farm. The maker and operator of this early proton magnetometer, Martin Aitken, later became Professor of Archaeometry, Oxford University

4 Excavation, Totterdown: an example of a carefully-sited single cutting to answer a specific question arising from field survey, here one of several such trenches designed to date the low boundary banks of what proved to be a Roman field system. The section shows the buried ground surface on which the boundary developed in this area of clay-with-flints; with Delling Copse top left and, to the south, the slope down to Overton Down, the Kennet valley and the western edge of West Woods in the far distance.

5 *Fieldwork in West Woods on a length of Wansdyke formerly in East Overton, now in West Overton parish. Here, this post-Roman earthwork has a low, incomplete bank on the south and a relatively deep ditch on the north (left). The wood further left, Brickiln Wood, is pitted with quarries, as much as 6ft (2m) deep, dug into the clay-with-flints capping the chalk. Though no old trees are visible, this general area has probably been managed as permanent woodland since at least the late Saxon period.*

6 *Marlborough Downs as viewed from a balloon to their south-west. The tree clumps are on Avebury Down, just this side of Overton Down; the further woods right centre of the picture are respectively Totterdown Wood, Delling Wood and Wroughton Copse on Fyfield Down. The West Kennet Avenue, its stones partially restored, runs across the foreground.*

7 *Overton Down experimental earthwork as completed in July 1960, dug into and made of upper chalk. It is designed to provide the opportunity for a long-term study of how a bank and ditch change through time when left alone, and has already produced interesting information on environmental and archaeological matters. The experiment is timed to end in 2088, by which time the earthwork will be scientifically priceless. It has already been designated a Site of Special Scientific Interest (**10**).*

8 *Valley of Stones, Fyfield Down, showing a relatively undisturbed field of sarsen stones, sandstone remnants of a former sea-bed which have drifted down the slope from the right, probably in wet and muddy conditions at the end of the last glaciation. The profile of this now-dry valley, with its steeper north-facing slope on the left, is characteristic of the local chalk-country.*

9 A recumbent, tabular sarsen stone, behind Delling Cottage on Totterdown, which has been carefully split into a first block ready for removal and then abandoned. This is a rare example of the stone-cutters' methods actually surviving at this stage of the work.

*10 Fyfield Down from the air, viewed from the east in very dry conditions, with Delling Copse top left. The broad light brown marks, left and centre, are the two branches of the old main road from Avebury to Marlborough; that at the bottom is a race-horse training gallop. The thinner light marks are the parched, north west/south east lynchets of rectilinear prehistoric fields, also reflecting the direct sunlight from the south-west which is simultaneously caus-ing the other sides of the fields to cast shadows. A good example of a complete field is left centre; otherwise much of the pattern is broken up by the parallel ribs of medieval cultivation, clearly visible top right. The lynchet excavated (**col. pl.14**) is the one just camera-side of the circular blotch in the centre of the photograph; the blotch itself is the filled-in crater caused by the explosion of redundant Second World War ammunition.*

11 *Sarsen stone on Lockeridge Down with a dish-shaped hollow and grooves on its upper surface, presumably made by Neolithic stone axes being polished and sharpened on it. The hollow has worn across some grooves. The surviving surface of much of the stone, which formally stood upright, is also polished; the further, western part of the stone was split off and removed in the early thirteenth century.*

12 *Cup-marked sarsen stone, Totterdown, probably decorated in the second millennium BC when it stood among contemporary fields.*

13 *Excavated section through a prehistoric boundary ditch, Lockeridge Down. Its bank is to the left, whence has come most of the lower chalk filling. The ditch cut through, and the bank overlay, traces of occupation including Beaker sherds of c.2000 BC. The central ditch filling of dark brown soil is interpreted as mainly wind-blown soil deposited in the later second millennium BC; and the horizontal line of small chalk lumps across its top as a surface when the by then slight linear depression was in use as a trackway early in the Roman period. The ranging rod is 6ft (2m) long.*

14 *Excavating prehistoric field boundaries, Fyfield Down. The cuttings across lynchets on both sides of the same small, rectangular field showed remains of a drystone wall which had been added, probably in the first century AD, at the field edge to accumulations of soil representing cultivation over at least the previous two millennia.*

15 *Medieval ridge-and-furrow on the southern part of Overton Down as viewed from the air in winter looking west towards the Ridgeway. The slight undulations are in East Overton tithing, 27ft (8.5m) wide, and superimposed on Roman and prehistoric landscapes. The prominent earthwork in the centre of the picture is a double-lynchet trackway cutting across prehistoric fields and respecting site Overton Down XI, top right; the late Roman site Overton Down XII is left centre; the long Roman village, Overton Down South, lies either side of the fence across the bottom of the photograph (Chapters 5 and 6).*

16 *The complete skeleton of a prehistoric male, 5½ ft. (c 1.68m) tall, in his twenties and buried with knees flexed and facing south on site Overton Down XI, probably soon after 2000 BC. The burial overlay the flexed skeleton of a child with a Beaker (**colour plate 31**) but was not itself accompanied by any grave-goods. Its knees and ankles rested on sarsen stones, like 'cushions', and 11 flint nodules, here picked out by their shadows, had been carefully placed from the crown of the skull down both sides of the body to a point level with the feet. The shape formed by the flints in plan was 'cloak-like', reminiscent of a shroud.*

17 *Excavated building probably dating between 800-600 BC on Overton Down site XI, viewed from the west. The narrow slots are where wooden walls once stood, here defining the large central part and southerly annexe of structure 'a' on* **34**. *Of the three visible pits, that on the left cuts the wall-trench of the later building 'd' and that on the right, in its own little rectangular structure and interpreted as a cess-pit, is illustrated in the next photograph.*

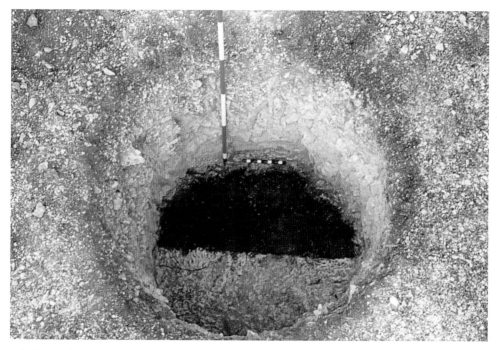

18 *Excavated pit, site Overton Down XI, as located on* **34** *and* **col. pl. 17***, structure 'a', showing the black deposit on its base, here half-removed to record it in section. The scale is in feet.*

*19 Down Barn cottage and area, Pickledean. The scrub on the skyline, top left, marks the site of a rare single burial mound; site Overton Down XI lies just down-slope of it, and the position of site XII is lower still, marked by the sarsens immediately above the ridge of the cottage roof. The Down Barn Enclosure lies just beyond the bushes on the left; the Overton Down South Roman village lies either side of the hedge line running diagonally towards top right (**colour plate 15**). The nissen hut was the remnant of a Second World War searchlight battery, here being used as the excavation camp kitchen and dining room, while the grass in the foreground is fallow on what had been the northern edge of one of East Overton's open fields.*

*20 Excavation of late Roman barn, site Overton Down XII, the southerly of the buildings making up pair 'b' on **40**. Viewed from the north east, the remains show the badly-robbed nature of the building immediately under the modern turf*

*21 Excavation of late Roman building, site Overton Down XII, the northerly of the buildings making up pair 'c' on **40**. Viewed from the north, the excavation had by the time of the photograph removed most of what remained of the stone-footed building outlined on **40** and the workers were investigating and recording the evidence for two underlying timber buildings*

*22 Lower sarsen stone of hand-mill as found in position up against the footings of the east wall of late Roman building 'a' on **40**, site Overton Down XII (**38**).*

23 *Later thirteenth-century buildings, Raddun, Wroughton Mead, Fyfield Down, the two easterly ones shown on **42** here viewed from the north during excavation. The two buildings, end on to one another but with separate walls in the middle, were cut down into the southerly slope so that the further one, probably for oxen and/or sheep, was stepped below the nearer one, badly robbed on its east.*

24 *Former manor house, East Overton, despite all the changes to it since 1567 recognisably the same building as sketched during the Pembroke Survey. A western wing across the foreground here has disappeared but the largely modern wing, centre right, perpetuates the position of its counterpart. The position and proportions of the main part of the house suggest not only that it is basically the Elizabethan building but also that that itself was probably a modification of a large medieval hall. Ironically, the thatch which strives to give the house an air of authentic antiquity is wrong; in 1567 the roof was of large diamond-shaped stone tiles.*

25 Long barrow and other early features on the ridge west of Lockeridge village, from the air in the dry summer of 1995. The green field with the parch-marks was called 'White Barrow' in the late eighteenth century, suggesting the barrow mound was known to be what it is and was then being ploughed over; it is now but the slightest of rises on the ground. Showing up are its ditches of c.4000 BC, the circular ditches to the right of flattened burial mounds of c.2000 BC and a bit later (though one of them might be of the windmill recorded here c.AD 1800), and the rectilinear ditches of what looks like an enclosed late prehistoric/Roman settlement (perhaps the 'enclosures on the ridge' which gave the village its name). The hedge climbing the hill diagonally right and neatly passing round the far side of what would have been an obvious landmark, the group of round barrows at the end of the ridge, is on the line of the AD 939 boundary of the East Overton estate.

*26 West Woods long barrow, Fyfield, one which if treated like that above Lockeridge (**col. pl. 25**) would also have been reduced to a couple of marks on an air photograph. As it is, apart from one late nineteenth-century digging, it survives splendidly, with its large mound, clearly defined side ditches, and causeways at both ends. Its future well-being would look even better were the trees on and around it cut down, their stumps and roots encouraged to rot and the consequential vegetational 'flush' regularly cut down.*

Left: **27** *Milestone on the north side of the 1743 toll road, now the A4, between Overton Hill and the Bell Inn. Its much-weathered facet, facing south-west into the prevailing wind and rain, just about still tells the eastward traveller that there are only four miles to go to Marlborough.*

Below: **28** *Knap Hill from a balloon early one morning, looking south into the Vale of Pewsey from just south west of Shaw in West Overton. This hill-top enclosure of the fourth millennium BC clearly shows the interrupted nature of its bank and ditch, on the ground as well as from the air. This characteristic method of construction, also evidenced elsewhere on some of the other earliest structures beginning the long process of modifying the British landscape, might suggest that initially this site was intended for agrarian and ceremonial rather than military functions.*

29 *Avebury: four of the great blocks of tabular sarsen stone which may well have been hauled from Fyfield or Overton Down in the middle of the third millennium BC. They were erected as part of the south-western arc of a complete circle of similar stones put up around the inner lip of the huge ditch enclosing an interior containing ceremonial and doubtless sacred structures. The ditch, and its outer bank, are on the right; just off to the left is the southern entrance into (or exit from?) the circle, one of four roughly at the cardinal points of the compass. In the centre on the southern skyline are more standing stones, there forming part of the megalithic avenue heading towards the River Kennet and the Sanctuary on Overton Hill.*

30 *Silbury Hill from almost directly above, showing, despite the ledge around its top (diameter c.100ft, c.28m), its dome-like profile figured in evening shadow on the grass c.130ft (39m) below.*

Left: **31** *Beaker from flexed child inhumation, site Overton Down XI, overlaid by the adult inhumation illustrated in* **colour plate 16.** *The pot itself is of a familiar shape but rare overall decoration; its date is controversial, but c.2000 BC is unlikely to be far out*

Below: **32** *West Farm, West Overton: the north front of the new farm-house built c.1820 or a little later by 'the coming man' in local affairs, Mr Pumphrey. He replaced his home in the medieval manor house opposite Lettice Sweetapple's house in West Overton village street with this fashionable small country mansion in its own grounds immediately outside the west end of the Saxon village. Behind it was a model farm, now replaced by the functional structures in the background. Pumphrey enhanced his privacy by facing his house away from the street and out across the water meadows; he reinforced his seclusion with a high garden wall which is not intended to be looked over.*

Dene. Its oval plan and two side ditches were strikingly similar to those of the one in Barrow Copse. We checked our historical maps: a late eighteenth-century one named the field containing this discovery as 'White Barrow' field. Well, at least we now had a ready name to hand for this new barrow: 'White Barrow' it shall be. That it should be called 'White' on the map strongly suggests that what was known to be a barrow was under plough and appearing as a white, chalky bump about the time of the French Revolution (**colour plate 25**).

We should have predicted its existence; but we had not then looked at the distribution of long barrows as a whole in this area. Once we did so, it was immediately apparent that their distribution was not accidental. They were spaced out in a meaningful pattern, each barrow being just over a mile (about 2km) from its nearest neighbour. We cannot know what was in the minds of those who placed these mounds so carefully around their landscape, but we can immediately spot the 'gaps' in the pattern where barrows should have been if the pattern was completed. The Lockeridge Dene barrow falls fairly precisely into one such gap, and we are now looking for its counterpart in the 'gap' to the west.

Another 'prediction', this time with a settlement, 'worked' up to a point in this southern landscape. It concerned the curiously-named Lurkeley Hill, though we did not expect to end up there. We merely projected south of the river the pattern of late prehistoric enclosed settlements, such as OD XI, about 1500m apart recorded on the northern downs. This indicated that a similar settlement might have existed right in the middle of West Overton's open fields among the strips of Lettice Sweetapple's holding (**58**). An intensive search of the area showed that, though she was cultivating land ploughed in prehistoric times, Lettice had not fortuitously farmed on top of a 2000-year-old settlement enclosure; but we did find what we were looking for a further 800 yards (750m) to the south on Lurkeley Hill.

So, by using a model and not being too rigid about it, we had found what was probably the major downland settlement south of the river in the early centuries of the first millennium BC. Though, like those on the northern downs, it probably did not last long, it had a sequel — just like the Headlands site we looked at in Chapter 6. There, the enclosure was crossed, arguably with deliberation, by the Anglo-Saxon estate boundary of the tenth century AD. On Lurkeley Hill, another length of the same boundary comes up from the south before making four right angle turns, west, north, west and north. Now we know why. It was avoiding the prehistoric enclosure, by passing along its southern and western sides; but you have to know that the enclosure was there to appreciate the point. Now, nothing is visible; and the map is blank. But, clearly, that enclosure was there as an earthwork when the boundary was defined (**55, 61**).

A little further south the same boundary also respected some early fields. On Boreham Down, beyond the southern edge of the permanent medieval arable, prehistoric fields had survived into the tenth century AD well enough for the East Overton charter to describe its route from Hursley Bottom north westwards as *'thaes weges to thaem hlince'* ('the way to the lynchets'). The last word refers to the accumulation of ploughsoil along a field edge. Indeed, these same fields survived another thousand years, long enough into the twentieth century to be recorded by the Ordnance Survey and also to be incidentally recorded during the RAF's air photographic coverage of the country in the mid-1940s. They had been respected by the medieval estate boundaries, again suggesting, as we have already seen on Lurkeley Hill, that these boundaries, first documented in the tenth century AD, probably originated much earlier. The area of these early fields was presumably not forested while they were in cultivation and their area has not been re-afforested since; nor do their remains extend back into today's woodland. It very much looks as if the present northern edge of West Woods is more or less now as it has been for two, perhaps 3000 years (**56–7**).

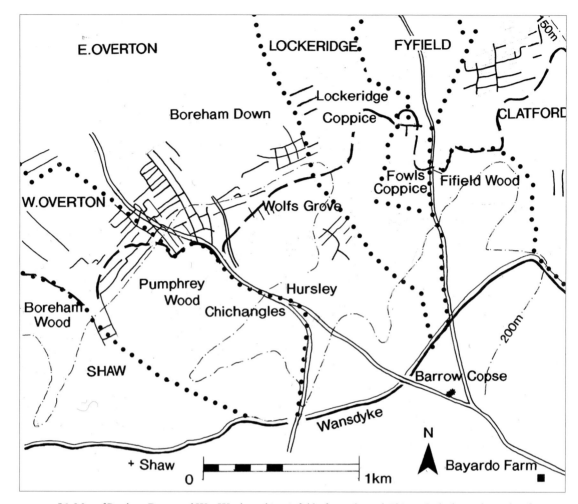

56 Map of Boreham Down and West Woods: prehistoric fields, forest edge and tithings. Only the northern edge of the woodland is shown (thick broken line). The tithing boundaries are dotted. The blocks of surviving prehistoric and/or Roman fields respect both.

Yet, as on the downs, we are missing the settlements here in the south for the last centuries of prehistoric times. Nor are we the first to notice this. Colt Hoare, as so often, had got there first. 'The hills in the angle formed between Wansditch and the Bath road leading to Marlbourough [that is, our southern area of Fyfield and Overton],' he wrote in his *Ancient Wiltshire*, 'are thickly covered with barrows and British works, but of small proportions ... I fully expected to have discovered some towns of the Britons; but ... I was not fortunate enough to discover the actual spot on which that people had settled'. So where were the people living? We just cannot have a population of perhaps 1000 people going missing for 500 years. But perhaps all of us have been asking the wrong question, 'where?' were the settlements rather than 'were there any?' Maybe our parishes were largely empty of people in the last centuries BC, the land given over to sheep, cattle and possibly, if we may anticipate the present, horses. The chalk-cut horses prancing round the edges of this area, north, west and south, may not just be pretty pictures.

Another feature which has caused much speculation in these southern reaches of Fyfield and Overton is Wansdyke, one of the largest and best-known of early boundaries in the country (**colour plate 5, 27**). Now more properly called East Wansdyke in our area, it snakes beneath the trees across our southern landscape. Its name in the tenth century AD — which may well not have been its original name 400-500 years earlier — was 'Wodnes dic' (or variants). Woden was, of course, the pagan Anglo-Saxons' principal god. It may have been built for him, not least because other Woden names like 'Wodnesdene' occur nearby, suggesting that some form of pagan cult centre existed. It seems more likely, however, that the earthwork was ascribed to him by later people who did not know who had constructed such a great bank and ditch or why it had been built. They therefore ascribed it to one of the giants of the mythic past. Modern understanding is not significantly more advanced.

Wansdyke crosses miles of open downland to the west before entering Overton to pass along the north edge of Shaw medieval village and through West Woods. Its ditch is on its north side, as if expecting attack from the Marlborough Downs. Its bank is a fine upstanding earthwork on the downs but mostly only a few feet high, and clearly unfinished in places, through West Woods. Two apparently original gateways through it occur along the southern edge of the woodland. In the tenth century one was called '*Eadgardes gete*', the other '*titferthes geat*'; both bar access to the south across old tracks ascending from '*ers lege*', the modern Hursley Bottom.

Wansdyke itself is undated, though bracketed in time between a Roman settlement which it overlies and Anglo-Saxon land charters, like that for East Overton of AD 939, which refer to it. Its most plausible context is about AD 500 when it could have been

57 Breach Cottage, Lockeridge: modern trees and house but with a name marking the place where, on the edge of West Woods, a clearing was made into the medieval forest towards the small settlement of Fosbury.

built either as a defence against the threat of Anglo-Saxon invasion from the Thames valley or, afterwards, as a semi-military political frontier of the British following their successful stopping of the Anglo-Saxon threat at the siege of Mount Badon (wherever that was; but unlikely to have been very far away). Whatever its exact function and date, three things about it stand out: it was built by Britons; it required a considerable, co-ordinated communal effort to build it, probably in a short time; and it quickly became redundant and its purpose forgotten.

The manorial farm at Shaw was actually built on it. This clearly suggests that, whatever that purpose was, it no longer applied when this new focus of settlement emerged, probably in the late Saxon period. The point is particularly striking in a settlement area where boundaries abound; people using it did not regard Wansdyke as one of them. Shaw straddled the boundary between two medieval administrative areas, called the Hundreds of Selkley and Swanborough, and between two ecclesiastical parishes, Overton and a detached part of Alton Barnes. Archaeologically, it was, and

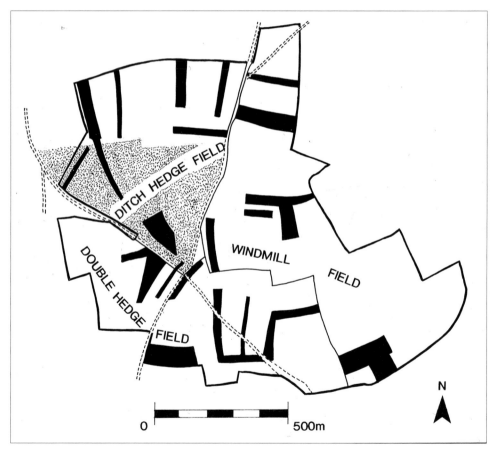

58 Map of the three open fields of West Overton, showing the lands of Lettice Sweetapple (solid black), taken from Map C, The Common Fields, of the manorial map, 1794. Although her strips were scattered in all three fields, clearly some consolidation of her holding had already occurred. At Enclosure, the whole of her holding was consolidated into one block of land, shown stippled in the former Ditch Hedge common Field — but apparently never actually enclosed (70).

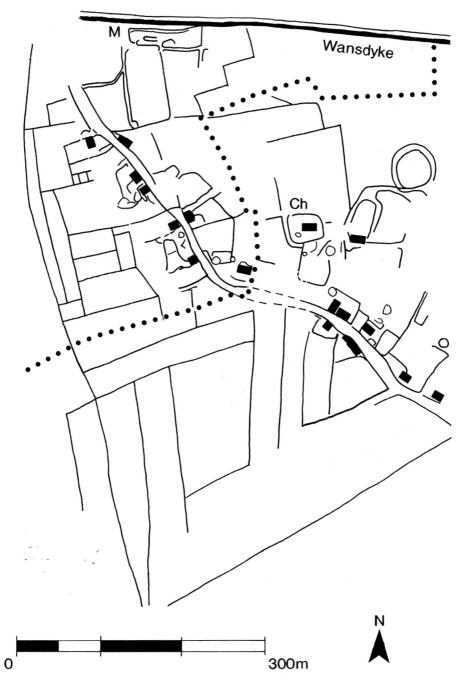

59 Plan of Shaw deserted medieval village showing its full extent, not necessarily all occupied simultaneously and clearly, like modern West Overton village, compound of two elements. Only the more northerly part was in Shaw, without a church but with the old manor house perched on the back of Wansdyke; the more southerly, with the church, was in Alton Priors. East of the church were probably prehistoric earthworks. The whole settlement lay astride one of the main tracks descending off the downs into the Vale of Pewsey. Of 17 potential buildings shown in solid black on the basis of field evidence, only one, the church (Ch), is certain; but each part of the village could well have consisted of three or four farms only.

to a certain extent still is, a fine site, with its earthworks clearly defining the shape of the central part of a deserted medieval street village. From air photographs, maps and field survey, we have been able to restore Shaw village to its full extent though probably, as we have already seen with other villages, this spread of earthworks overall represents a changing shape and size over the 400 or so years of its life. Its heyday is likely to have been in the thirteenth and early fourteenth centuries, though people were certainly living in the village in 1086. They are likely to have been occupying the place in the preceding centuries too, as well as in Roman and prehistoric phases that we have already noted.

A lonely place in the late twentieth century, Shaw was probably quite busy 700 years ago, for one of the few main tracks from the Kennet valley to the Vale of Pewsey passed along its central street. Perhaps that is why it is there. The street now looks like a shallow, flat-bottomed ditch winding between the sites of houses and gardens which once lay to either side. If the whole site was simultaneously occupied, perhaps up to a hundred people could have been living here about AD 1300. The village itself was last referred to in 1377 when it contained only three poll-tax payers. Perhaps it had become within a generation the totally deserted site which, some 500 and more years later, has excited the attentions of historians, archaeologists and a Marlborough College schoolmaster.

On the north side of the central street was a small embanked enclosure containing a low, oblong mound. H.C. Brentnall, a master at Marlborough College, thought these earthworks might be the site of a church and churchyard he knew of from medieval documents so, in 1939, he trenched the area. Our own investigations in Fyfield and Overton owe a great deal to Mr Brentnall but his *forte* was as a local historian using documents and a good eye for the land rather than in digging. Nevertheless, his afternoons at Shaw with schoolboys and other helpers were spent on one of the earliest archaeological excavations of a church to be carried out in England. Understandably, it was not technically a very proficient operation, but it did confirm the existence of a church with a simple ground plan. Its internal shape was based on a double square (33ft x 16ft; *c.*11m x 5m). The building had been almost completely robbed of its masonry and architectural fittings, lending credence to the local story that Shaw church had been removed southwards to Huish down below in Pewsey Vale. This seems to have been about AD 1400, after a life of perhaps little more than a century.

By the time that happened, northwards at 'old' West Overton another 'lost' church, this time on the homeground of Lettice Sweetapple, may well have already been missing for several centuries.

9

Start by the church

The site of a church, 'at the *chiricstede*', is the rather surprising starting point of West Overton's Saxon charter. This priceless document of AD 972 contains one of the very first written references to the land of Lettice Sweetapple, 800 years before her time.

Like many parishes in this part of England, the first time the village appears on parchment is in the Old English of a Saxon land charter. These charters were legal documents detailing a grant of land. Their intention was to define, usually reinforce the definition of, the boundaries of an estate either in the normal course of land management or, more usually, before the land was granted from one person to another. Characteristically, the event was a gift from the king or other lord to the church, for example a nearby religious house, or to a favourite thegn. Of course in order to prevent disputes and so that the next owners knew what they were being given, the boundaries of the newly acquired estate needed to be carefully described. At the time, therefore, 'beating the bounds', as the process came to be called later, was a deadly serious business as a jury moved from what was for them one obvious feature in the landscape to another.

60 The Ridgeway south to Overton Hill, here descending the long slope from Overton Down through a landscape which remains basically unenclosed even though the track itself has recently been fenced in. This is not 'the oldest road' by any means, for here it overlies, and is therefore later than, Roman fields and the Roman road to Bath; but it was in use as a pathway in later Saxon times. Some of the burial mounds of the Seven Barrows lie to the left in the middle distance. The photograph cannot capture, however, one essential element of this landscape — the sound of skylarks.

The unintended effect for us was that not only were boundaries defined but that whole stretches of countryside were, at least to some extent, characterised. The main text of the charters can take a modern investigator around the perimeter of the estates, always in a clockwise direction though there was no standard starting point. Indeed, locating the starting point may well be an initial difficulty for the modern boundary-walker. We are going to try following in the footsteps of some Anglo-Saxon jurymen here, using what they wrote as clues to guide us round 'their' countryside.

Three Saxon charters have survived for our area. In 939, 15 hides of land at East Overton, a 'place known of old to the local inhabitants as Bank Farm' near the river Cynetan, were granted by King Athelstan to Wulfswyth, a nun at Winchester. Just over thirty years later, King Eadgar granted ten hides of land at Vuertune (West Overton) by the Cynetan (River Kennet), to lady Ælflæd, who was probably also a nun but this time at Wilton Abbey. The third plot of land which interests us was at the northern edge of the large southerly estate of Oare which pushed right up against Wansdyke in Fyfield. This land was first granted in 839 to a certain Aethelhelm, but then re-granted in 934 by King Athelstan to Wilton Abbey. Both Oare and West Overton, therefore, became part of the wealthy Wilton Abbey estate in the 930s. East Overton, on the other hand, came under the domain of the Bishops of Winchester.

61 The Ridgeway south from Overton Hill, moving into and through an enclosed landscape with hedges as it passes The Sanctuary on the right of this view and the most southerly of the 'Seven Barrows' on the left before dropping into the Kennet valley towards the 'paved ford' of the West Overton charter. The estate boundary defined in AD 972 runs along the west side of this track, now marked by the thick hedge and still the parish boundary; or is it that The Ridgeway developed alongside a boundary already long recognised? The same boundary can be seen zig-zagging as a hedge-line up Lurkeley Hill in the far distance while The Ridgeway veers away to the right above Langdean Bottom.

*62 'Long Tom', the tallest standing stone in the area, on Fyfield parish boundary with, now, Preshute civil parish. It stands on its low bank, ditched on the west side, between Fyfield and Clatford Downs, heading towards the scrub on the skyline which contains both a megalithic barrow and an incomplete millstone (**17, 19**). Marking the boundary between medieval estates, tithings and manors, the boundary itself is certainly over a thousand years old. It is, therefore, very tempting to see the 'menhir' as Saxon or even older, being used as a convenient marker by later boundary-makers. The long straight run of the boundary bank here suggests, however, that it may well represent geometrical tidying up of open and rather featureless downland at Enclosure (1815). The cut of the stone, similar to that on field gate-posts hereabouts, does not discourage such thoughts.*

These charters, with their descriptions of streams and ponds, paths and fords, flowers and trees, can provide a reader possessing some imagination with a vivid picture of how the landscape was farmed, where people lived and worked, and what sorts of plants and animals were occupying the countryside. Such documents give an unparalleled insight into late Saxon England, its economy and embryonic industries, its farms and homes, even its beliefs. The inclusion of heathen graves, barrows and standing stones (**62**), along boundaries which have divided the territories of English communities for many centuries (**24**), also gives us a brief insight into the local folklore of those Saxon peasants. *Wodensdic* and *Wodensdene*, *mere grafe* and *hursely* are all places with eerie, heathen connotations — the ditch and bank built by Woden, the great god of Germanic legend; while 'pond grove' and 'horses' clearing' suggest worship of other deities. Suddenly the image of a winter evening in the Great Hall appears, with children huddled around a fire, listening to the story-teller recounting the days when demons, druids and thunderous gods stalked the land around Overton long before their Christian salvation.

A church is usually the fixed point in a village around which houses come and go, but no sign of a church has ever been uncovered in the first Saxon West Overton (Chapter 7). Careful analysis of the charter, however, tells the landscape detective where to look for clues in the fields hereabouts. As the preceding point on the charter is Lurkeley Hill and the next one a 'streetford' across the Kennet (**55**), the 'churchstead' would have had to have stood at the western edge of the estate on the boundary now marked by the Ridgeway (**61**). At first we thought the site may have been near the sixteenth-century Orchard Farmhouse, probably in the area of the original village of West Overton, but the early maps from the Record Office pointed to a spot a little further south. At the junction of The Ridgeway and the track called Double Hedge Way which travels across the downs to West Woods, the cartographer of 1794 had inked in 'Church Ditch'. Caution has to be shown here, for this land may simply have been ecclesiastical. The reference certainly does not prove a church, let alone the Anglo-Saxon church we sought, stood here; yet such a reference might conceivably have caught an earlier memory, and the location itself appears promising (**58**).

The small church was presumably a simple wooden building in origin but possibly with at least stone foundations by the tenth century. It could have served the needs not only of the small community straddled along the Ridgeway, but also the travellers who were increasingly using this downland route in Anglo-Saxon times to journey, with their flocks, herds and goods, between the Thames Valley and the Wessex chalklands to the south. West Overton in, say, the eighth and ninth centuries could well have been a busy spot, the perfect place for a church to prosper, catering for pilgrims, weary shepherds, monastic staff on business, traders and warriors. The remnants of the church, wherever it stood, have not yet been discovered, even after an extensive aerial photographic search. Walking the fields after the next ploughing, though, may prove more successful.

The greatest reward of all for the modern explorer comes, however, when he or she sets out, with charter in hand, to trace these boundaries of a thousand years ago. The hackneyed sentence that 'The past is a foreign country' comes to mind for, although the landscape may be reasonably familiar, you are looking at it through the eyes and mind-set of a 'foreigner' from another time-country. So imagine our satisfaction at discovering that the charter's *Titferth's* gate actually existed at a gap in Wansdyke, the significance of which had not previously been spotted; and at suddenly stumbling across 'withypond' of the charter and finding willows still there. Another cliché, the one about walking in the footsteps of the past, literally becomes true (**63**).

Here we are working out what happened after Titferth's gate around the extreme south eastern corner of the East Overton estate as visited in AD 939. We wonder if they had some sort of sketch map as well as their vellum text. We used old Ordnance Survey 25 inch (1:2500) and 6 inch to the mile (*c.*1:10,000) maps; you can easily follow, on the ground but without even getting out of your chair, using one modern Ordnance Survey 1:25,000 map, New Explorer sheet 157. The 'gate' was at the south corner of Wells' Copse and Little Wood and at the west corner of Barrow Copse where a track passes through Wansdyke (SU 15406570). From the gate, the boundary travelled to the east side of the hedge at 'willow pond' (*withigmeres hege*) and then *suth on butan Aethelferthes setle on thone stanihtan weg*, 'south around Aethelferthe's dwelling to the stony way'. The pond lies just beyond the long barrow we met earlier in Barrow Copse (Chapter 8), and willows continue to grow there. Indeed, the species at Willow Pond might well be lineal descendants of the Saxon ones.

Locational exactitude is important, for the following point in the charter holds out the rare promise of being able to identify the site of a Saxon house of a named person, Aethelferthe — though we have not yet found it. The site lies somewhere high among (former) woodland on clay-with-flints. The place may have been near the end of the track from the clay pits (SU 15126527), where a settlement stood from the late eighteenth century until at least the 1930s. Or it may have been near Heath Cottages (SU 15586514), which was the home of Ralph atte Hethe 400 years after the charter.

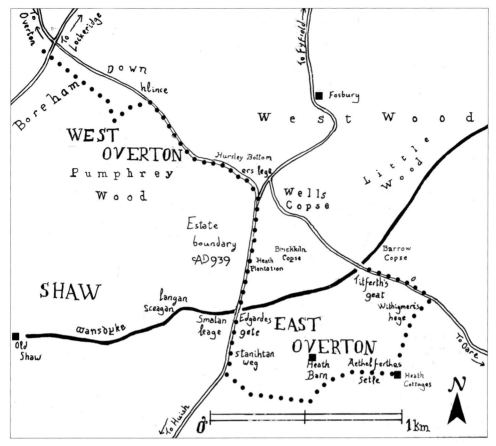

63 Map of the southern bounds of East Overton, AD 939, shown as a dotted line clockwise from 'Titferthes geat' to 'hlince'. Other points from the East Overton charter are named, as are some other features for the purposes of identification using a modern map.

The present parish boundary follows the tenth century one here as it turns west at Heath Cottages, and heads south along the edge of Heath Grounds and then west to join the track from Huish to Lockeridge (SU 14706514), the *stanihtan weg* of the charter. The 'stony way' suggests that this route was metalled, perhaps in a similar manner to the Ridgeway at the West Overton/East Kennet ford as described in the West Overton charter. So perhaps it was a busy way too, giving added significance to our identification of another gap through Wansdyke as another 'gate', *Eadgardes gete* (SU 14786548). This break in the ditch lay near *langan sceagan*, the long wood, and *smalan leage*, the small or narrow lea. The boundary then continued east of Pickrudge and Pumphrey Wood, *thurh scyt hangran and lang thaes weges to them hlince*, through Chichangles — wonderful name — along the path to the lynchet. At the time *scyt hangran*, the 'wood on the steep hill-side', marked the western edge of Savernake. Over the generations this tongue twister was modified into a word the people of Wiltshire found easier to pronounce, *Chichangles*. In the early nineteenth century, in another act of etymological vandalism, the new tenant farmer replaced this lovely name in favour of 'Pumphrey Woods' (*see* 'Lettice Sweetapple in fact'). We are happy to restore *Chichangles* to its rightful place on the map (**56, 71**).

This last *wege* would seem to be the hollow which skirts the northern edge of Pumphrey Wood, now a public footpath and once the tithing boundary. Evidence of its later, continuing role as a boundary exists in the form of low, round-topped marker stones inscribed 'HM' (Henry Meux) along its edge. The Meux Estate owned much of the land hereabouts in the later nineteenth century. The boundary now reaches open pasture (SU 143666) where in the tenth century there may have been arable. A thin strip of hedge, baulk and trees remains today, possibly the remnants of what our predecessors saw as *hlince* along what became the northern edge of *Allen's Higher Ground* on the 1794 map. We are fairly confident that what they saw was indeed a lynchet, not of their fields but of the prehistoric field system on Boreham Down (Chapter 8). We are leaving them here but just remember that the Saxon boundary inspectors continued in like vein for some 15 miles (24km) as they meticulously checked and sought agreement on each and every point. We have only followed them for 2-3 miles (*c*.4km).

Every feature must have stood out in some way to have been chosen as a fixed point and the charter makers must have expected the particular tree, home or stone to remain a lasting element of their countryside (**62, 64**). In fact, as we have now seen, some of these elements have indeed lasted a thousand years, quite remarkably if you think that such survival has been achieved in a busy working landscape. But then, many of the charter points have gone on being used throughout that time, and usefulness tends to be a rather better recipe for survival than redundancy. Look, for example, at field edges. Fairly ephemeral, you might well think, but throughout the charters the boundary-men

*64 Boundary bank and ditch between the current civil parishes of Fyfield and Preshute but actually at least a thousand years old, being the probable northern edge of the Saxon Fyfield estate. It is the same boundary as in **62** but further uphill where it additionally defined East Overton Cow Down on Fyfield Down, reflecting the fact that the Bishop of Winchester's manors of Fyfield and East Overton were run together for much of the medieval period. The bank and ditch carefully touches but does not go over a megalithic burial mound rising under the gorse bushes to the left. The trees on the skyline are around Old Totterdown, half a mile (1km) north-west.*

65 'Plus ça change': 'Lamb's path', AD 939, photographed 1157 years later in 1996. The description comes from the East Overton charter; the place is on the north side of Pickledean, opposite Down Barn. Down Barn Enclosure lies to the north west, just beyond the hawthorns to the left; Overton Down South Roman settlement is to the right of the hawthorns top right (see 37).

were using headlands, baulks and lynchets as their markers, meaning that they regarded them as not just visible but likely to be permanent. Some such features were already old — lynchets from prehistoric fields, for example — so they had good reason for their belief; and posterity has proved them right, for still today edges of their contemporary fields function as boundaries in the modern landscape. We have just seen one on the southern edge of Boreham Down. A particularly striking one is up behind North Farm, north of the Kennet, where a boundary marked by a mere headland in AD 939 is still the permanent and fixed boundary between two of the major farms in the area (**36**).

Because such boundaries were effectively permanent, however slight their physical nature, hedges grew on them, some still visible today like the one just mentioned between the two Overton farms. In some cases the boundary was probably making use of landscape features that already existed by taking its line from one to the other. But in others, it seems most likely that stone, clay and gravel pits, ponds and chalk quarries were dug along the boundaries, characteristically placed with precision so that each party was able to draw on the natural resource.

We can fill in parts of the landscape with other activities too. From the beautifully enigmatic description of *lamba paeth*, we know that sheep were taken along what we now call Pickledean to and from their grazing on Overton Down (**65**); from charter evidence, we know a dairy farm existed on Fyfield Down in the tenth century, a fact now supported by some pottery evidence from Raddon (Chapter 6). By the river a salt-house, or *Sealt Ham*, stored fish and meats. The River Cynetan was crossed by a series of fords, some of which are still passable today as many remained in use until only a few decades ago. One, as we have already remarked when we began by the church, was a *straetford*, a paved ford, for heavily-loaded waggons to cross — or was it for an army? There was a big battle close by soon after our tenth-century charters were so helpfully compiled, and skeletons were dug up in this vicinity in the nineteenth century (**60–1**).

Another unanswered question concerns landscape features which were already old when the charters were drawn up. While more recent constructions, such as the Roman road and Wansdyke, are merely mentioned in passing, the more ancient features of the landscape, especially barrows, crop up time and again. This regular appearance cannot be simply explained by their prominent nature — surely the Roman road and Wansdyke were at least as obvious as landmarks? Nor can it be explained by the apparent ease with which the boundary could be sighted from one barrow to the next. In one outstanding example in East Overton, the boundary runs between two barrows causing the modern hedge to turn through a right angle three times to accommodate the old division. We have noticed the same thing on Lurkeley Hill where, in that case, the boundary jags round a prehistoric settlement enclosure (Chapter 8; **55**).

Barrows and other prehistoric landscape clutter along the Anglo-Saxon boundaries must have been included, self-evidently in one sense, because they were at the periphery of estates. But this begs the question: that clearly was the situation in the tenth century but, if Bronze Age burial mounds and ditches were already at the edges of these estates in the Saxon period, when did these estates first emerge? We keep having to ask that question, and the evidence always points backwards, earlier than late Saxon, sometimes earlier than early Saxon and suggestively to Roman and later prehistoric times (**24, 55–7, 63**).

People, collectively and even individually (like Mr Pumphrey), inhabit the landscape and make things happen in it. In studying Anglo-Saxon charters you meet the people who are probably the first named ones in a locality. From Overton four, no doubt prominent, local characters emerge. We have already met three of them: *Aethelferthe* of the missing house and the distant stone (**17a**), and they of the Wansdyke gates, *Titferthe* and *Eadgarde*. The other is *Colta*, whose name was attached to a *beorg*, or barrow, in the ancestral landscape up along the Ridgeway. Let us now meet some other, non-charter residents.

10

Peopling the land

Of the tens of thousands of individuals who lived, worked and died in the Overtons, Lockeridge and Fyfield, only a few dozen, rather than hundreds, have names which come to us from before AD 1500. And yet, through a combination of systematic pursuit of groups of people, families and individuals through the documents, and luck, we have been able to assemble and then infer quite a lot about some of these random survivors.

We know of them mainly through documents to do with land. The medieval system of tenure and land management created the need for considerable bureaucracy, notably land charters, records of property transactions, accounts and lawsuits. Through the documents which have survived from that morass of vellum and paperwork, we are able to meet some of the people who contributed to the making of the land of Lettice Sweetapple during the Middle Ages. Indeed, after careful study of the surviving written sources, along with maps, aerial photographs and hundreds of hours spent walking the parishes from end to end, we can now confidently identify where many of them lived. More interestingly, the search has also meant we can unravel some of the complex histories of these people and their lands, not least because, though they are dead these six centuries, their land still lives. We have come to know the Knights of St. Quintyn, the unhappy tenants of the Knights Templar in Lockeridge, the nuns of Wilton Abbey and Richard of Raddon. These are brief versions of their stories.

MILES OF GLOUCESTER AND THE KNIGHTS OF ST QUINTYN

About sixty years after the completion of Domesday, Miles, grand-nephew of Durand of Gloucester, granted his estate of *Locherige* to the newly formed Order of the Temple (see Lockeridge in Chapter 7). The Templars' acquisition of Locherige, with all the woodland, pasture and meadow noted in 1086, was a foundation donation to their new estate.

Miles, like most nobles of the time, was an absentee landlord, however, so the day-to-day management of his manor had been left to Ricardi de Sancto Quint, his knight. St Quint was a man of means himself, and may well have lived on any one of his other nine estates; but he was nevertheless a touch peeved at losing part of his management portfolio to an upstart group of semi-religious do-gooders. He demanded from Miles land in exchange for his loss. Miles agreed; and so, it seemed, St Quint's Lockeridge holding was exchanged for land outside the area.

But we could not locate this new Quintin land, and we lost track of the knight himself. Then we came across another grant to the Templars dating from the 1250s, a hundred years later. This described a donation of a dwelling-house and a meadow by a certain Richard Quyntyn, resident of *Lokerugg*, Wiltshire. Surely this man had to be a descendant of the St Quint disrupted by the creation of the Templar estate in the mid-twelfth century? Furthermore, this Richard's land was described as being leased from the Bishop of Winchester, suggesting very strongly that he was living on the estate mentioned in

Domesday, then too leased from the Bishop, which had been held by the Earls of Gloucester, the lords of St Quyntyn's forefathers. We had our story. When Miles gave Lockeridge to the Templars, he granted St. Quint his neighbouring estate, the one he leased from the Bishop in East Overton in exchange. St Quint had not in fact left the area; he had simply moved next door. So, the St Quyntyn family lived very close by, but could we say where ?

Richard Quyntyn's grant to the Templars consisted of an 'entire meadow' with a messuage, or house, yard and other 'appurtenances' in the 'town' of Lockeridge. Part of the estate, therefore, must have been close to the Kennet because meadowland can only be by the river. The Quintyn's had other meadowland as well. At about the same date, Thomas de Macy granted a meadow to the Templars. It was described as the one 'that Albert my father bought at some time from Richard Quintyn ...[which] lies besides the meadow of Walkelini Suith'. But we could only ponder that two meadows hardly constitute a two hide estate worthy of a knight and regret the fact that the last reference to the Quintyn family was apparently in 1275.

Part of their estate, however, had by 1316 passed to John of Berwick, a man who was acquiring much woodland in the area. This part remained intact and, descending through John of Fosbury, by the early sixteenth century had been acquired by Richard Benger. Like all the land hereabouts, it was then acquired by the First Earl of Pembroke at the Dissolution of the Monasteries. The Earl, rather like William the Conqueror some 500 years previously, ordered a Survey to be carried out of all his newly acquired lands. His men reached West Overton in the autumn of 1566 and set about recording in detail each household, its possessions, livestock and buildings, and how much it paid in rent. And, quite unexpectedly, there in the Survey, 300 years after the last reference to the family, is 'Quyntons lands ... ' and a cottage at 'Fortesbury ... known as Hardings [but] once called Bengers' (**57**).

Thanks to this entry, we now know that St Quintyn moved his family into West Woods at the southern edge of Lockeridge after his estate was granted to the Templars. There they must have built a farmstead and cleared land to cultivate their crops. Three generations later, however, the meadows were gone. Richard Quintyn sold one for cash to the up-and-coming de Macy family and, for his soul, granted the other to the Templars. Without meadowland to support their animals, and isolated in the woods with only restricted land on which to grow crops, perhaps life became too arduous as the farm began to lose its agricultural viability. Like the desperate family across the valley at Raddon, the last straw may have come after the series of very wet years in the early 1300s. The Quintyns, once loyal Knights to the Earls of Gloucester, simply sold up and moved on — a familiar enough story, though not usually thought of in knightly terms.

Today the area these early pioneers cleared, farmed and abandoned is next to Fosbury Cottages, evoking the name of John. It looks a very unhistoric spot; yet to it, by niggling away at family history in topographical terms, we can locate with accuracy a two-hide Saxon estate, recorded in Domesday, leased by the Bishops of Winchester and given to the Knight St Quint in the 1150s when the Templars arrived in Lockeridge, assarted in the later twelfth and thirteenth centuries, owned by numerous people in the fourteenth and fifteenth centuries, and surveyed in 1566 by a new owner who, naturally, wanted to know how much rent he could receive from it (**55**).

THE TEMPLARS AND THEIR TENANTS IN LOKERUGG

The Templars were a quasi-religious military order originally set up to protect pilgrims to the Holy Land, but their operations tended to go a little further than that in the land of the Infidel where Christianity itself was somewhat in jeopardy. Such a benevolent undertaking, however, like overseas charitable work today, requires sponsorship from the supporters back home. Much of this support came in the form of land grants by the nobility. Between 1141 and 1143, the Order acquired one of the two-hide Lockeridge estates, we suggest that based on Lockeridge House. In 1155–6, it acquired downland up at Rockley where it built its preceptory. With another grant about the same time, by the end of the twelfth century the Templars were established with a remote place of worship and a three-hide estate called *Lokeruga* to support it and their community. Present-day Lockeridge may well be on the site of a brand-new village laid out and built on the flat ground between the two Anglo-Saxon settlements of 'Lockeridge' (House) and Dene in the middle of the twelfth century (**55**).

The Templars set about transforming the small estate and settlement that had once belonged to Miles. Their aim, of course, was to make Lockeridge produce a surplus so that the brothers' economically unproductive lives could be supported and the good work of the Order continue in the East. First, though, they too needed to know what they possessed. In 1185 each Templar preceptory in England was ordered to carry out an Inquest. Every parcel of land they owned was scrutinised, all rents duly noted and each obligation recorded. Lockeridge was, in turn, assessed. The estate contained at least 48 acres of arable and pasture, and six acres of common land, and was shared by nine *cottars* paying a total rent of £2 14s 10d. Two of these cottars also rented crofts, which suggests outlying or isolated homesteads. Between them, each owed 2s for an area of assarted land. We have already noted the Quintyn family busily assarting simultaneously. So we can infer that in the late twelfth century Domesday woodland was being cleared under the direction of the Templars. Indeed, Breach Cottage, at the very edge of Lockeridge Copse, illustrates the process in its very name: a break had been made in the forest edge and a settlement planted (**57**).

The Templars, in the 40 years or so since Miles' donation, had already forced change on to the stubborn peasants of Dene in their new, planned 'villa de Lokerigg' (Chapter 7). The Inquest of 1185 detailed the customs of service the tenants were expected to deliver. In general, as we shall see, the terms were similar to those expected of Richard of Raddon working a few decades later on the higher downs for another ecclesiastical landlord. Each tenant of the Templars who held a five-acre tenancy at Rockley had to provide one woman each day to milk, shear and wash the sheep. In return the tenant daily received a loaf of bread and 'half a whey' produced from the milk, as well as 2d for cutting and milking the sheep. At Lockeridge, everyone who held one virgate of land had to give three *stricas*, or strikes (a unit of measurement) of corn at the Feast of St Michael and 1d for each pig each year, as well as supplying two men in the autumn for three 'boon works' to feed the Templar brothers.

Such arrangements could have been written for any peasantry in southern England at the time, for all they do is spell out the detail of the message that 'the landlord rules OK'. But in Lockeridge, almost incredibly given the commonly-held image of feudal stability through rigid containment of tenants' aspirations, rural unrest was not only simmering but was expressed. In a classic example of early collective bargaining in a popular dispute, the tenants together rejected the legitimacy of the obligations now articulated by their new landlord. They argued that many of their supposed duties had not actually been agreed and that new payments had simply been imposed by the Templars. The villagers were simply not prepared to accept them without discussion. It all sounds very familiar to us but is perhaps somewhat unexpected for the mid-twelfth century.

Even the clerk whose account we are following seems to have agreed. He commented that the fees were introduced 'when Osbert of Dover held the bailiwick' and had been imposed on the tenants 'through Alfred Cat. and Serichum White'. He further observed, however, that they had nothing to do with him, and what was he to do? — he was only the scribe after all. The Templars, it appears, were attempting to legitimise in writing customs which were probably a mixture of new and old, and not yet all formalised. The tenants were clearly alert to what was going on as their new and somewhat pushy new landlord tried to make the best of a good deal. Unfortunately, we do not know how the dispute was resolved; but we can note that, while the tenants continued for centuries, the Templars were dissolved in 1308.

THE NUNS OF WILTON ABBEY

A nun called Wulfswyth was given land in *uferan tun* (West Overton) by King Athelstan in AD 972. As a member of the community of Wilton Abbey, but perhaps outstationed at Overton, she was part of an extensive bureaucratic estate which came to record the highest rental receipts for a nunnery in the country in the thirteenth century. Two hundred years after Domesday, however, Wilton was on the verge on bankruptcy, in spite of generous royal gifts in the twelfth and thirteenth centuries. In 1229, 1252 and again in 1276, the tenants of Wilton were requested to contribute towards the Abbey's relief — rather as if late twentieth-century mortgagees were asked to bail out the Halifax plc.

This demand would have been particularly unwelcome in West Overton, for its resources, in comparison to those of its neighbours, were fairly limited. The growing financial troubles of the nuns at Wilton Abbey are in sharp contrast to the growth and prosperity of the neighbouring estates of the Bishop of Winchester. In fact, right across Wiltshire, indeed much of southern England, the middle decades of the thirteenth century appear to have been a particularly prosperous time. So why were the well-endowed nuns of Wilton Abbey in dire straits?

The answer lies in their lifestyle. Apparently their discipline was lax and they enjoyed a more lavish standard of living than the monks of St. Swithun's who farmed Fyfield and East Overton. To help the Abbey, the abbess was granted permission between 1221 and 1246 to take over a hundred trees per year from within the royal forest of Savernake. Yet this was still not enough to cover their costs of living, so the community, instead of retrenchment, foolishly plunged into illegality to sustain their version of a life of holiness. They decided to begin assarting areas of the forest on the quiet, as well as reclaiming land for tillage without royal permission. Such activities could not possibly go unnoticed for long and, inevitably, the Abbess was charged with illegally obtaining timber and was fined. Today, the result of the Abbey's desperate attempts to balance its books is reflected in the arable land around Park Farm and is remembered in the name of Abbess Cottage. Both lie at the very south-eastern tip of what is now Fyfield parish in what was a detached part of West Overton manor. Bearing in mind what was simultaneously happening in adjacent Lockeridge, the woods were certainly alive in the thirteenth century (**55**).

RICHARD OF RADDON

The people we have come to know best, however, did not live in a grand religious house or even in one of the villages; nor did they mix with nobility. They lived on Fyfield Down in a small, apparently isolated farm called Raddon between *c.*1220 and 1318 (described in chapter 6). One person, Richard, we know by name but, though at least three generations lived on the farm, his successors remain shadowy. Richard was the first generation of occupants; we like to think of him — though this goes further than the direct evidence — as an ambitious pioneer father, perhaps succeeded by a son who enjoyed prosperous days of expansion in the later thirteenth century. The bottom then fell out of this familial world, though whether it was Richard's grandson who abandoned the farm in or about 1318 we do not know.

Richard of Raddon was a contemporary of Richard Quintyn, Thomas de Macy and Richard Sokemond of Lockeridge. He would also have heard about the Abbess of Wilton's covert activities in Savernake across the valley and been familiar with the Templars' street-village at Lockeridge. His church was St Nicholas in Fyfield and his lord the Bishop of Winchester, acting through the Prior of St Swithun's.

The Raddon farmstead may have been physically isolated in some senses but the downs were busy at the time. Across them immediately north of Raddon ran the upland route of the great west way from London to Bath and Bristol, now called 'Green Street' (**47**). Especially in the wet winters, when the Kennet flooded its bank, many more travellers than normal took this way and would have needed help from time to time. After all, how many ox-teams were available across those deserted downs? And then, repairs to vehicles: Richard and his sons had wood and carpenter's tools, and perhaps they themselves could also carry out emergency blacksmithing — on ox-cues and horse-shoes, for example. And with their large house and several buildings, who knows but that an emergency bed and breakfast could not be provided? All this is speculation, of course, but it is not fantasy, for there is certain archaeological evidence to be explained and we know how difficult cold and driving rain, never mind snow, can make conditions across the downs (**6, 46a**).

Across those downs too moved the huge manorial flocks with their shepherds. The Templars' shepherds, milkmaids and herdsmen would have passed Richard's homestead high on the downs on their daily journey between Lockeridge, Rockley and the downland pastures. To the east, what had been downland for centuries was now being ploughed up, so workers came up from their homes in the valley to work there too.

Also from time to time the Knights Templar, in retirement now and beginning to look a little portly, would re-fight their battles of long ago, lumbering at the great grey stones as if they were Saracens. Still, such fantasy was to be encouraged, for it meant a need for horses, armour and weapons. Sometimes, when the stables at Rockley were full, the Templars asked Richard to house their horses in the paddocks at Raddon; he could also mend their suits and sharpen their swords. In return they gave him knightly accoutrements like a pair of spurs and a powerful, armour-piercing arrow.

With all this activity, Richard was seldom alone, but at least the reeve, appointed by the Bishop to ensure the smooth running of the estate and the regular payment of dues, was not continually on his back. In fact, the reeve had little to worry about. Richard was a trustworthy man who could be relied on. His farm was perfectly placed to look after the vast manorial flock, and now that the downland east of Raddon was being ploughed, Richard also had the lord's oxen to house and attend to. His barns stored food for the beasts, as well as some of the harvest, and at shearing time, the sheep were carefully penned and kept safe from attacks from predators (**42–4, 68, colour plate 23**).

Richard's special function and duties within the manor of Fyfield meant he required a separate entry in the manorial accounts. The Latin document, a bulky roll of calf-skin called a custumal, reads as follows in translation:

Richard of Raddon holds half a virgate of arable for which he must look after his lord's two ox-teams at his own expense from devastation by wolves and from theft of thieves and robbers. He must drive the said teams to ploughing and bring them back when the ploughing work is done. And whatever damage the said ox-team commits, the said Richard is responsible. Moreover he will look after the field under corn between Hill and Aist. If any damage is done there, he shall pay sheaf for sheaf, until it is safely stored in the barn. And daily in autumn he shall supervise the reapers and hand over them a sheaf, which they shall receive if the land is properly reaped. And when he carries the corn he shall himself collect the remains of the ears with a rake; and in carrying the lord's hay, he shall have a rake to help. He must concern himself with the ploughing for the field of the oxen, in seeing that it is properly ploughed. In the ploughing taskwork he shall himself help with the ploughing and sowing. He ought too to keep safe the two downs of Hackpen and Raddon, when they are hedged off from the cattle and to answer for the damage from outside. He must give the seventeenth hen as Cherchsett at Christmas and 200 eggs at Easter. He is to help at the lord's sheep-shearing in packing up the fleeces and shall receive one fleece and one lamb when they are separated from their mothers. And he is to have one cheese and one acre of corn at his free choice from the cornlands, except for the one plot set aside for the lord's choice.

Perhaps Richard's responsibilities were so carefully set out precisely because his tenement was distant from the manor house but he nevertheless enjoyed a certain amount of freedom and a good deal of comfort. He probably received some sort of extra income in kind from downland neighbours and travellers. More formally, the shepherd at Raddon was exempt, for example, from having to submit his grain for grinding at the bake-house in the village, so flour was ground at Raddon and bread baked in an oven built into the end of Richard's old house (**45**). When the horses or oxen needed new shoes, or when the buildings needed new nails or latches, or when new tools were needed, a smithy would come up from the valley. At Raddon he might have re-used the long, flint-lined rectangular fire-pit as a furnace to heat his irons for working on his portable anvil. Richard himself may well have planted a small wood of hazel, for his hurdles and firewood, and oak, for building work, just uphill from the farm. It flourished on the local clay-with-flints over the chalk bedrock and is today a prominent landmark called Wroughton Copse.

To eat with the Raddon family would be to eat well, for their living seems to have been better than most were enjoying in the village. Bones from the archaeological excavation, rather than documentary evidence, show us that they kept and ate sheep, cows, pigs, goats and hens, and hunted and ate wild duck, partridge and deer. The household itself was quite well-equipped, with well-built furniture, latched shutters and a padlocked door and fine-glazed pitchers from the Clarendon kilns just outside Salisbury and cooking pots from Newbury along the Kennet valley. The ladies had rings, brooches and decorated buckles. In a pit under the floor was a security box, a chest with a lock and key. The earthen floor was regularly swept clean, especially around the new fireplace and chimney, and the rubbish was chucked outside along the rubble walls or dumped in the top of an old pit.

Richard died some time in 1248 but Raddon continued, perhaps with Richard's son now the manorial tenant. Sheep-farming prospered in the second half of the thirteenth century, bringing more wealth to the great Winchester estate. Clearly Raddon was not an obscure or insignificant downland farmstead, but a vital element in the mass sheep farming that was such an important part of the commercial activity of this particular manor. Indeed, with cultivation nearby, it was a key element in the whole manorial economy. It was one of three *berceriae* on the manor, along with *Attele* (now Hillside Farm) and *Hacan penne* (west of Overton Down Barn). Raddon and Hackpen provided permanent winter housing for the large flocks of sheep; they consisted of stone and timber-framed structures within a ditched and hedged enclosure, more or less as was found to be the case by excavation (**41**).

In 1309, a great storm took the roof off the Raddon sheepcote and hay had to be bought in for the sheep because of the bad winter. Flooding throughout 1315, 1316 and 1319 severely damaged crops, and wheat prices rose steeply. The good times at Raddon were suddenly in the past as worsening weather and its economic consequences exposed the essential marginality of its situation as a place sustainable for human habitation. Sheep and cattle continued to graze the downland pastures for centuries to come but, sometime late in 1318, and probably after yet another harvest failure, the family walked out of history as they abandoned their farmstead, leaving it to crumble in the wind and rain.

PART III: A HISTORY

11

Up to Avebury

WHAT WE ARE ABOUT

So far we have explored, largely on a geographical basis, a quite small area of landscape contained within the modern parishes of Fyfield and West Overton. We stay in the same place but now bring in an additional dimension, time. Here is the start of a straightforward narrative about the land of Lettice Sweetapple. We follow the good tradition of telling our historical story by simply beginning at the beginning, here taken as about 10,000 years ago. We come up to the early nineteenth century AD, so we are two centuries short of ten millennia.

Our story, we stress, is an interpretation of the place and what we know about it; strictly speaking, it is not a history, for we have not kept to facts alone. Further, it is only one of many interpretations; we could easily have written another story, and what follows must not be taken as, in any sense, definitive. It is an informed guess, a highly selective interpretation. Our attempt to narrate a coherent, consecutive story about one small place turns out to be, perhaps inevitably, a brief essay in assertion rather than argument, for in the interests of narrative we bypass awkward questions, avoid uncertainty and use imagination. For this and the next two chapters, the story is the priority, as we tell of how it could have been rather than limit ourselves to ascertainable fact. That said, all our imaginings are based on a piece of evidence somewhere.

It is an obvious point but, in a story of this sort moving forward through time, the 'dates' are largely derived from outside our parishes until the tenth century AD.

THE FIRST 4000 YEARS (C.8000-4000 BC)

By *c.*8000 BC possibly, by 6000 BC certainly, people were successfully living on the land which, thousands of years into the future, was eventually to become the parishes of Fyfield and Overton. These people, in most respects exactly like the modern inhabitants except hairier, were much pre-occupied, even in a well-endowed area like the Upper Kennet valley, with the daily tasks of acquiring food. Such tasks occurred within the longer-term needs of the seasonal life-cycle which underpinned their way of life. Eight thousand years later few need to be too much concerned with the different foods the seasons can produce, because only a very small proportion of the local population, even in an agricultural area, now gains its livelihood directly from the land; but 6000-10,000 years ago, in contrast, most of the local community would have been dependent on that factor. Unless we grasp that fact as fundamental, not only to our Stone Age communities of *c.*6000 BC but throughout the thousands of subsequent years up to Lettice and the end of this story, then we cannot hope to begin to understand what was going on in Fyfield and Overton and their landscape.

Between 10,000 and 7,000 years ago, that landscape was clothed in trees. They and other vegetation flourished as the glaciers retreated to the north and as the climate became warmer. Indeed, woodland gradually closed in, creating deep deciduous forest in places, as it still is in parts of Savernake Forest. But that Forest is only a relic of a great spread of woodland which reached its maximum extent in these millennia. There were no Downs, for the open grasslands are not natural and were created much later. Now, the Chalk supported forest, wood and scrub, a good place to hunt, gather and collect. Early Overtonians found good hunting of deer, smaller mammals and birds along the forest edges in particular, a strip of land where they could also gather, so they noted, hazel nuts. But they had to search in the forest for one of their favourite foods, wild pig, though they had long learnt that the place to wait was among the stands of beech, especially in the winter when the mast lay thick upon the ground. They were finding it worthwhile, however, to cut and burn the curiously denser under-storey so that open glades were maintained as places where their prey was attracted by the Moon Goddess in exactly the way she had looked after her hunters since time began. And where the deer habitually grazed at dawn and dusk they noticed that the berries ripened better than in the forest itself. 'It must be something to do with the earth,' they observed to each other, 'Where the earth is cleared, there our food comes. The earth is good, the earth is fertile, the Earth is our Mother and our Goddess too.'

The valley was another rich resource, for it was completely undrained. Fed by fresh water springs bubbling all year, it was a soggy marsh with a sluggish river seeping through it, edged with willow, alder, reeds. Bird-life teemed; the noisiness of it all would probably offend twentieth-century ears, at least just after dawn, but it was music to the locals who caught birds for their meat, bones and feathers all the time, and took their eggs in season. Open water and pools, it was noticed, attracted fish, and therefore highly catchable birds like heron, so some of the women went down and cleared away the water weeds in special places while the men chopped back the overhang of Spring growth. The pleasure of 'fish-tickling' was added to the routine of the daily food-quest. The Upper Kennet valley, rich in a variety of natural resources then as now, would have been a better place to live than most.

It also possessed flint, lots of it, on the surface and underground. So the local groups of people could make their own tools — their fish spears, their arrows, their scrapers and knife-blades — without having to move far or trade. They almost certainly lived along the edges of the river valley, even out on 'islands' of gravel or mud in the flood plain. The riverside near Avebury, and just above the flood plain as at North Farm, were occupied, at least from time to time. They travelled too, on a seasonal round following prey but also revisiting places where food mysteriously regrew each year, things like mushrooms and chestnuts, fruits and berries. Some journeys were local as these hunters and gatherers moved along the forest edges at Shaw and Bayardo Farm or in the open woodland of Piggledean at Down Barn. But some were longer to more distant places across their 'territories' and beyond, though it was in truth only an hour's walk to the south to the very different ecology of the Vale of Pewsey. And the higher lands of the northern edge of the Marlborough Downs, and the different habitat of the Upper Thames valley just beyond, offered yet other resources from different habitats within a day's walk to the north.

People of the upper Kennet valley could take flint to the dwellers of these northern districts, as gifts and also in the hope of exchanging it for goods. Though only several hundred people lived around the south-western fringes of the Marlborough Downs, now their numbers were growing and the landscape was beginning to fill up. Beneath the routine and monotony, communities and their habitats were astir. Many of the best places for living, camping, hunting and gathering, for example, were long-known and much used; they were coming to be recognised as 'belonging' to one community in particular. The growth of a sense of ownership, and possibly also of a family 'belonging' to one area, were just examples of the more subtle changes taking place among people living off one area and within a lifestyle which were both experiencing changes too. Some were long-term, ecological and material; others were of today but sometimes of great local significance, as when the deer inexplicably disappeared for a season, as when part of the woodland became diseased, as when a great storm lashed the land, sweeping vegetation and soil off the slopes and down into the valley.

THE NEXT 2000 YEARS (4000-2000 BC)

The daily, seasonal and annual round continued in a landscape not noticeably changed from earlier millennia. It was not so necessary, however, to keep working away at and in the forest to stop it spreading and to maintain the glades; but it was recognised as a good idea to maintain the tradition, for clearing undergrowth and felling trees seemed to attract animals and improve the availability of collectable foods. Indeed, one of the families had made a special glade for the animals, not to kill them everyday but to protect them altogether from predators. Where they had tried the same thing up on 'the heath' near Bayardo Farm last year was now an extraordinary sight, with new fresh grass-spears and all sorts of flowers blooming among the hazel, thorn and oak shoots. Brambles were rapidly spreading around it. Clearing trees also produced trunks and branches which could be used, not just as fuel and shafts for tools and arrows, but to try out this new idea of building things. Certainly these new wood-framed shelters were useful in bad weather; but now there were other worries.

Strangers had been reported, camped on the local eminence at Knap Hill and elsewhere in the region. They seemed to like the high ground above the tree canopy but they had been seen running along the forest edges at Shaw and Piggledean with small wolf-like animals which they whistled at. They had already put fences up, as if they meant to stay, and kept some very strange animals indeed inside the pens: they tugged at bumps underneath some bony brown ones, which kept bellowing 'MooOO' as if in pain, and pulled the coats off some smaller, greyish-brown ones which looked and sounded particularly stupid as they continually bleated 'Bah! Ba-ah!'.

These new-people stayed, more of them arrived, and they started chopping lots of trees down and setting fire to whole areas of woodland and scrub. Some of the woodsmen wielded 'magic' axes, axes made of smooth pale green and pale grey stone quite unlike the jagged beauty of the local flint ones. A man who stood and watched the work occasionally carried a long, bright green stone axe which never touched a tree but before which, so it was said, whole woods obediently fell. After the felling and the burning, these newcomers did not wait for wild animals to arrive and be killed in these opened-up areas as the natives had learnt to do effectively; instead, and to the incredulity of the minds behind the pairs of watching eyes among the foliage, men and women came to the glade and killed one of their own brown animals with horns. They slit its throat, letting the blood soak away along a groove marked in the ground. Then they spent several days walking up and down with two bony brown creatures and a bit of wood, scratching the ground. After that, they did a sort of dance — or so it appeared — waving their hands about and scattering little brownish-yellow pellets on the soil. Finally, they put a fence around their cleared area, and went away, leaving a wooden 'stick-god' standing alone.

It was clearly all an elaborate bird-trap. When the birds flocked in, however, curiously children chased them away instead of catching them. These were strange and topsy-turvy times indeed, and clearly these newcomers did not know how to respect the land in the ways that the Old Ones decreed. Nor did they know how to catch a good supper. The locals turned up their rustic noses at these incomers and went off hunting, happy in the knowledge that they had nothing to learn from people who clearly were not knowledgeable about country ways.

After a few years, nevertheless, there were even more of these 'foreigners': they seemed to have made themselves at home and were inviting their friends to join them. Now there was always the smell of wood-smoke, and the lights of fires dotted the ever-longer, receding forest edge at night. Now, too, they started digging circles of long holes around their hills. Clearly the real locals could not go there any more, for to cross the magic rings was, it was said, certain death; but more and more of the new-people did, and it was frightening to see them in their hundreds, shouting at the sun as it dawned and the moon in the white-light of its fullness. Local new-people, now with their homes here, also gathered in some of their own places, where they had cleared some land or where they had seen a god. They danced and sang with their animals as they drank yellow-pellet juice. Then they started digging in these places too.

They knew they were being watched, and they found their work hard with so many large stones in the ground. Two of their men came down to the valley one day, offering one of the stupid animals and a basket of those yellowish-brown pellets to the 'natives' — who, in blind terror, killed them. The next day, lots of new-men came, killed some old men and women, tied up the young women and took them away, and drove the young men off to work for the rest of their lives in building great stone and earth monuments at what became known as Dillion Dene and Barrow Copse (**18, colour plate 26**).

The 'Overtonians' heard that similar events had occurred in neighbouring territories and that now nearly all the able-bodied men of the whole district, except for a few who had escaped into the forest, were slaving away heaving great stones. These had to be hauled across now open country into positions which seemed senseless — and of course no explanation was offered by the 'masters' — but which had to be exact on locally high ground in Kennet and on Walker's Hill. These megalithic mounds, it became apparent, were being carefully spaced out around the area, their exact position fixed by 'wise-men with a sense of place' who advised the area's first 'landlords'. Each megalithic mound marked a territory, its edge not its centre, so that each incomer had to pass the 'test of the ancestors' before entry. These boundary places were then dedicated to the Moon Goddess and the Earth Mother, borrowed from the natives because they seemed to work, joining the Ancestral Ones brought from Europe. Then could these sanctuaries of mortal and immortal spirits be used for great ceremonies on special days, and became ossuaries for the remains selected for permanent preservation from the descendants of the founding families.

Much of the landscape was now open and cultivated in patches, but large areas were scruffy with regenerating scrub. The mounds, though built on cleared and previously fertile land, were, of course, hidden in clumps of uncleared virgin forest. These were themselves 'holy', relict nature reserves belonging to the ancestors, now monumentalised for all time as sacred places of Mother Earth and an increasingly confident, self-conscious

Person Man. He was now very much guided by thoughts of ancestors and community, of a time continuum from what went before and may some day come to pass. In Fyfield and Overton south of the river, White Barrow marked the take-over of the valley by the new-ones who had now cleared its sides and were wondering what to do about the spreads of ash-speckled alluvium beginning to accumulate at the edges of the slopes. The megalithic mound by the forest-edge on 'the heath' reminded people that that was the boundary with the land of the proudly non-arable woodland people, a female-dominated group of hunter-gathers of mixed gene-pool and implausibly elaborate ethnogenesis. They chanted long into the empty night, believing their day was yet to come. They had simply disappeared by the end of the period.

This emergent landscape of the new-people was a landscape stripped of its old meanings. It could hardly be 'read' at all by the old survivors of hunting, fishing and collecting days, and in any case the children, whatever their ancestry, did not want to know and did not care. They saw and grew up in what to them was a normal landscape of visible activity, an exciting round of felling and burning, ploughing and planting, bird-scaring and harvesting. They liked their songs of the skies and the fields instead of those gloomy old ones about talking to the trees. The whole of life for young and old was punctuated by a succession of festivals and 'holy-days' increasingly given over to intense bouts of drinking, drug-taking and communal eroticism. And you could see the results: more new-people babies, more of the strange and forbidding forest cleared away each year, and more food more easily 'magicked' out of the marvellously technicolour fields each year. This was the future; and it worked.

So what had been a strange new landscape in olden times, so the stories told, became a familiar and desired landscape. It helped everybody get through the killer season of late winter and early spring; and it left energy and time to build ever greater monuments to the gods so that the seasonal circle of farming life became the cycle of sustained improvement in the quality of life. They had discovered its secret: the sun. When the sun shone, their crops ripened and they prospered; when it did not, they slipped back towards the bad old days. It really was as simple as that, however great the mystery behind the Solar Fact. 'Let us then praise the Sun God, husband of Moon Goddess,' they pragmatically argued, 'that they may look after us in their celestial risings and settings which control our seasons, our harvests and our very destiny.'

Overton territory had never been marked by a western boundary mound for, from long ago, it already shared in the special spiritual status of Overton Hill on the edge of great things beginning to happen a little further west. Some inspiration came from the north. Visitors came from that direction, following the easy 'summer way' along the foot of the downs or, in winter, along the crest of the high ground. But perhaps they just enjoyed the long-distance views now opening up. Beside the Way, the northern limit of Overton's territory was marked by the erection of the Great Stone, telling travellers that they were now entering an important place. But the people had misread the signs and the Stone lay down to become, as the gods wished, the Anvil of the Sacred Axes. This was a prestigious, high-status entrance to the place, far more honorific than an upright megalith which, after all, any place with half-a-dozen fit men could put up. And it was new, a new symbol to mark the beginning of the new and sacred landscape being created to bring the people and the gods together in harmony. To this stone came traders with their roughed-out stone axes, pilgrims with their light-weight decorative axes and, occasionally, great leaders with their polished stone blades of power — all wishing to rub or just touch their axe-heads on the holy stone. Here they paused, in expectation and to collect their thoughts, before entering the Great Landscape of the Gods (**colour plate 11**).

Women and men wrestled with this concept and its physical expression for centuries in the crook of the Upper Kennet valley. By *c.*2500 BC, every community hereabouts had its own sacred landscape within its territory, a landscape marked out with holy places for gathering, prayers and burial. Long mounds, though now full and rather old-fashioned, remained powerful places to intercede with the earth forces, but it was at local circles of stones and of wooden posts that the communities along the river banks offered obsequies to the Sky Ones and prayers with praises especially to the Sun God. They kept the seasons in order and on time, but they had to be asked properly for rain in the spring and for sun, lots and lots of it, in the summer. They had to be honoured so that they supplied that crucial dryness in the autumn for the harvest, the ceremonies of thanksgiving and the great fighting in the fields. Then was it that, in relief and thanksgiving, men showed off their worldly goods, fought for political supremacy, and made bids for power, wives and lustful companions of the passing night. The Sun God simply could not be thanked enough.

And so the idea of a great temple was born, itself inspired in the minds of the people by the gods of the skies. And every year for a century, and then another hundred years and another, every village for 50 miles (80km) around sent ten people to Avebury, not to labour but to worship through new labour as they worked in a great co-operative effort. The effort was continuous once started, day after day with routine and preparatory tasks, with two special periods each year, in June and September, when after careful planning the big jobs were done with concentrated muscle-power. Overton and Fyfield, important places, showed their status by sending two contingents, the obligatory levy in June and a voluntary group of the villages' strong men after harvest.

First, great symbolic groves in standing timbers were created on the Kennet's bank. Then a huge ditch was dug to define the successful holy place, for harvests were good year after year. And then, to ensure prosperity forever, the temple was rebuilt in permanent stone as the whole landscape was dedicated to the gods and goddess of sky and earth, and especially to the Sun God, in one great act of planned, communal worship. Twenty miles (32km) across the southern downs, similar communities were building similarly, on a smaller scale but with a greater intellectual sophistication which emphasised the oneness of Husbandry with Nature through the metaphor of the Static Circle of the Moving Stones; for they had rationalised their life-way and their belief, now in one, single great Sun-God, alone save his chaste and humble servant Diana.

A natural cult centre also developed around the spring that fed the fertile little river Og flowing through the Kennet valley. It was looked after by a group of families beginning to call themselves the 'Sil' who were already talking rather grandiosely of marking the place in some impressive way. On the boundary between them and the 'Overtonians', the beginnings of a shared ceremonial centre emerged on Overton Hill, at first with unmarked graves and ritual pits and then with sarsen stones as in the tradition of the ancestors. People came to be buried here and a temple became necessary, as pilgrims began to come from far beyond the local territories; so an elaborate wooden structure was begun and dominated that western skyline as the period ended. It was called 'The Holy Place', later 'The Sanctuary'.

From the west, on the eastern skyline of the 'Sil', it looked puny and old-fashioned compared to the great simulated forest groves that were created along and spanning the river Og. These were places for inward contemplation rather than expansive views. Yet the urge to go up, to tower above the waters and the trees, to be up among the powers of the sky, was a powerful one. The concept of the Millennial Mount took shape (**colour plate 30**). From all around people began to wrestle with what began as a labour of love and ended as an expensive nightmare — the huge and unintentionally empty Sils' Burg, an earthen mound intended to represent the dome of the millennial skies heaped over the green of the fragile Earth. It was timed for completion exactly 2000 years after the First Arrival, according to the priests and their magic calculations, but in fact it was never finished.

Things began to career out of control at Avebury and its surrounds as the ancestral millennium approached. Too many people, first devoutly and then opportunistically, took the soft option of holiness instead of the hard work of farming. Circles of wood or stone, or both, began to appear all over the place. The Kennet's banks became crowded, the river became polluted with ordure and sanctity; the sense of holiness was diminished as much of the area came to look like a building site. Private 'praying grounds', some erected by incomers in a rush, competed with the social ones, built properly and more slowly in the traditional ways of the people. Calls for more voluntary help were sent out as, all too slowly, the bulk of the Stepped Dome of the Kennet spring-head, began to heave itself above the swamp: estimates of the amount of material and man-hours required were already shown to be wildly inadequate. Some began to doubt whether it was wise to lose five acres (2ha) of such good, well-watered pasture, all ready for grazing in the early summer, to such a grandiose monument which seemed increasingly to reflect political stubbornness rather than spiritual vision. For twenty years, every man and woman in Fyfield and Overton laboured with their kin from the vernal equinox to the feast of Baal on steps three and four at Silbury, and no-one tilled the fields. Grain was imported from less holy places, though the elders warned that weakness could come from over-dependence on strangers faraway.

With everybody local occupied, contractors had to be brought in to fit into place one of the principal elements of the grand design: the processional Path of the Good Ones linking two of the old temples, Avebury and the Sanctuary, into a new holistic entity. It was still hoped that volunteers would construct the equivalent Path towards the Westering Sun but, though one or two stones were put up, it was never seriously started. To the east, returning to familiar ground, the people of Overton tried to rebuild their end of their Path in their spare time over a generation, while their neighbours looked after the animals and children in both Overton and Fyfield; but still no-one ploughed and where old men recalled fields they now saw a thick litter of long grass, thorn-trees and uncoppiced hazel.

Contractors had been hired to build an avenue of large sarsens with just a spread arms' breadth between their outer edges. Accustomed to building earthen banks and ditches on Thames valley gravels , they never mastered the skills of placing great stones in solid chalk. They were shown the 'Giants' tear-drops', the great tabular sarsen stones of Dillion Dene and Clatford Bottom; they were guided along the Line of the Walking Stones across Overton Down and down Green Street to Avebury's eastern gateway; and they paced out with the elders the route they had to follow in erecting the Avenue of the Petrified Procession. It ran from Avebury's southern entrance, south west along the west side of Waden Hill and the east bank of the Kennet towards the construction site of Silbury Dome, round the southern end of Waden and then due east to the foot of Overton Hill, finally edging south eastwards across the slope and straight into the Sanctuary. It was explained about the problem at this eastern end: that the Holy Place was being refurbished by another firm of contractors who simply had no idea what the original had been like or for.

The Avenue contractors, however, had also underestimated both price and effort. So, after building the first few paces on the correct alignment south west from Avebury, they took a short-cut with the rest, hurriedly bringing a much attenuated Avenue along the easy route east of Waden Hill then swerving south east to Overton Hill, using stones hastily dragged up from the adjacent river bed but far smaller than specified. So, in the end, like so many *grand projets* in the future, the creation of the Great Landscape was never really accomplished.

But much worse was the result of attempting it at all, of worshipping gods who, in the end, failed to deliver. Far better to have listened to the wise men. About the end of this period, around *c.*2000 BC, the Avebury area, including Overton and Fyfield, suffered the unpleasant experience of 'systems collapse'. The land had become unproductive, the people were exhausted and the suppliers of external aid no longer sent their oxen trains of grain. They had found other, more profitable markets for their products and, in any case, the ultimately highly-centralised and undemocratic economic system which had driven the obsession with sanctity could no longer, no matter what the threat, raise any tax. All unwittingly, the result was that the foundations of the area's much later claim to be a World Heritage Site were laid, for by *c.*2000 BC, the landscape, exhausted, disused and largely depopulated, was already markedly a landscape of redundant monuments, littered with ruins. But the trees did not come back (**colour plate 6**).

12

To the end of the old world

THE LAST 2000 YEARS BEFORE THE ROMANS

Into this run-down landscape of the Avebury area two details represent the start of profound changes which were to set the agenda for the next two millennia. West of the great henge monument itself, the chalk subsoil beside an already ancient ceremonial mound at South Street, and the tops of its silted-up ditches, were scored by parallel grooves made by a small wooden plough, or ard. This was in use during new, rigorously systematic cultivation of a well-drained flat area, previously lying idle. Up on the higher ground east of Avebury, a small, new cemetery was dug on Overton Down. In it were buried a robust man, a woman and a child with a pottery beaker; they may have been a family. The ard-marks at South Street and this unremarkable funerary scene on Overton Down marked an attitudinal change towards the Earth and a rebirth in use of the land (**66, colour plate 31**).

The small local communities of the Avebury/Fyfield district were once more recharged by thoughts that things could and should be different. Radicals among them were re-inforced in their advocacy by newcomers who moved in from other parts of England. The Overton Down robust male was one such, arriving and marrying a local girl. He and others brought with them new energies and new ideas about flint technologies, pottery, managing land and, above all, a new material called 'bronze'. This they magicked out of those rare but long-known metal ores, copper and tin. They kept themselves to themselves, these friendly strangers, but their obvious power and skills readily gave them an authority. Before long, they were established in small settlement centres which included their own graveyards both on the Downs — they had at least three such places on Overton Down alone — and in the valley, as on the patch of river gravel at Lockeridge near where they lived. They were the acknowledged leaders and soon their quiet but authoritative influence could be seen as the landscape was tidied up, re-activated and organised in ways which everybody could understand.

They marked out the land for different purposes. Most of it, in a return to fundamentals rather than the siren-calls of religiosity, was given over to food-production, this time not on an ownership basis but by function; for they understood the magic of the soils did these people who taught others how to make decorated and elegant reddish pottery. High on the Downs, they said, crops will not grow well but the cold, stiff soil will welcome the cattle and sheep for their summer grazing; so they marked off the pasture-land along its southern limits by showing others how to dig a long ditch between the Rivers of Kennet and the larger Og away to the east (**21, 24, colour plate 13**). 'And south of this ditch,' they said, 'nearer to where you live, you must lay out fields instead of just making clearings which you walk away from after a few years. These fields will be enclosures which will last, built side by side so that one edge serves two fields in a very efficient pattern; and these sides will be marked by stones cleared off the earth so that you can tend that earth. And all these sides will line up together in a gigantic pattern stretched symmetrically

66 Prehistoric male inhumation, site Overton Down XI, probably of c.2000 BC and interpreted here as indicative of major changes in attitudes to land and in the organisation of land-use beginning about this time.

across Mother Earth, each field facing into the path of the sun to and from its zenith.' And so was the downland organised, and a shift in local belief brought about. People, perhaps without realising it, went back to the basics of the Earth Goddess, supported by a Sun God who did his daily duty but no longer held sway over human affairs. They were now much more under the control of pragmatic humans neither expecting miracles from nor shifting responsibility to some unsubstantiated Other (**16, 25, colour plate 10**).

This was shown by the landscape itself, especially by the systematic enclosure of fields. An invisible line had been drawn across the downs, stretched between two tall posts and with sarsen stones to mark its way roughly towards the setting sun; and then another line across it towards the rising sun after calculations by the leaders. 'But the important thing is to spread the fields out *towards* the sun, to warm your Mother Earth,' they said. Year after year, the fields spread, block by block, across the landscape in the warm and dry centuries around 1500 BC. Each year, every man along the valley settlements was given an area to break in, and was helped by the men with their sighting poles and marking sticks to place them correctly in the grand and efficient design. And it was a sensible way of doing things, they found: everybody knew where their plots were and how to get to them, and so did everybody else. They could all get on with the real work of producing food, manuring and ploughing their conveniently-sized fields with the little ards that everyone now had, occasionally going too deep and biting into the surface of the chalk beneath the thin soil; and then taking the crop in the autumn without any ambiguities as to who took what.

At the beginning, some new fields were sanctified by carefully placing a burial mound at its corner; other intakes in the new system respected the existing burial grounds. Later, however, the management of this new landscape of enclosure placed limits on the expansion of ancestral cemeteries and the creation of new ones. The lands of the ancestors came to be confined to the rough grasslands, some scrub-covered, around the margins of the blocks of arable fields (**23**). On Dillion Down, where a new intake on second-choice land was eventually slotted into the overall pattern, the Great Mother's help was permanently invoked by patiently indenting a special stone with symbols of her potency (**colour plate 10, 12**). This also was a new idea brought in from the North, and Fyfield was the only place to have such a stone. Its communities, and those in neighbouring Overton, were growing in size again, and looked down from the Downs into the wooded valley, thinking that it might be a good idea to move there to live by running water and release more of the chalkland for their developing agriculture.

But, within the technical and managerial efficiencies of the system, slowly things were changing yet again; and, so the elders sensed, for the worse. It seemed to rain more often throughout the year, and often for longer. The winter wheat sometimes simply failed to germinate in the soggy ground of wet November, even on the chalk; the spring cereals sometimes found it difficult to get away in February and March, for the soil was wetter and colder for longer than they liked. The harvests of July were becoming a fond memory; sometimes now it was even September before the ears were ready to take. And, inexplicably, the soils in the fields seemed to be becoming thinner, for the ard-tips were constantly biting into the chalk now — and sometimes snapping as they snagged on a flint or buried sarsen. Indeed, despite the years of stone-picking, there seemed more flints and sarsens on field surfaces than ever. Then the awful truth dawned: the rain, the provider of goodness, was taking their soil away, washing it downhill off the open downland and leaching out the goodness which centuries of manuring had carefully maintained.

The response was both immediate and long-term. Many of the existing field edges were revetted with sarsens; some fields were laid out anew with new field walls built into their structure. And whole blocks of fields were re-aligned within a slightly-different axial arrangement designed to fine-trim the whole system so that soil drift down-slope was halted or at least minimised. Scattered homes and farmsteads appeared in an evolving pattern within their field systems which were now at their maximum, spread on both sides of the Kennet valley, stretching high on to the downs even where covered with clay-with-flints and up the north-facing slopes south of the river on to the heavier soils edging the forest on Boreham Down. This massive investment yet again of human effort into the landscape at a time of growing population and less benign climate led people to live among their fields, not just to warn off birds and other animal predators but to protect their fields, their land, as much as their crops. People felt that somehow they could do better if they were close to their work and livelihood all the time.

And this pattern had coalesced by *c.*700 BC into a carefully distanced distribution of several communal, enclosed settlements: three or four among their fields on each side of the river in the Overton/Fyfield area which was by now supporting a local population of a thousand people (**21**). They were living in round timber houses, some of considerable structural and even architectural sophistication; and they were pursuing a deeply religious strain in their agrarian life-style, involving intercessions with the powers of the Earth and highly complex relationships with selected animals and their iconography. With such large numbers using the local land and its resources, however, and with pastoral needs to be met as well as those of the arable, the landscape was moving towards being fully-utilised; within the technology of the mid-first millennium BC, it was reaching the limits of its carrying capacity. Perhaps strangely, therefore, the potential of the near-unique local resource of sarsen stone for building was not carried through from the fields into three-dimensional and domestic or funereal uses.

As pressure developed on the landscape, so social and political tensions grew. Rivalry developed and, ostensibly in the interests of protecting people and crops from raiding and theft, the local situation was resolved in a draconian way which left its imprint on the landscape for all time. A further elaboration of the process of centralisation led to the emergence of just three or four locally-dominant *equites* or war-lords, men who could boast of the allegiances sworn to them and point to the stretches of land in which their power of territoriality held sway. Fyfield and Overton, perhaps unfortunately, fell right between the 'territorialities' of three such lords. Their centres of authority, all fairly rapidly converted into impressive head-quarters by large ramparts, palisades, ditches and elaborate entrances, developed at the hill-forts of Barbury, Oldbury and Martinsell, respectively a few miles/kilometers to north, west and south-east. As a result, people were moved out of their enclosed farms 'for their own safety', as the lords' men woodenly said to any protesters, and then forced into servitude either at or in the political shadow of the hill-forts in return for the 'safety' they were now told they enjoyed.

Their former settlements were divided up so that the actual land they occupied could be put to 'better' use. This was part of the larger division and re-organisation of the area into 'hill-fort territories' in the seventh-sixth centuries BC. The lands of (what were later to become) Fyfield and East Overton north of the river and west to the Ridgeway went to Barbury, with West Overton and Shaw as well as Kennet and Avebury going to Oldbury; everything else south of the river, including the valuable resources of West Woods, owed their allegiance to Martinsell. With the management of land and people now possible on such a large scale, the rationale of resource-use was no longer merely the needs of the immediately local community; things were planned on a territorial, sub-regional basis. The arable fields of Boreham Down, for example, were kept under cereal by the lord of Martinsell, who did not have vast areas of open land on his estate. In contrast, the traditionally arable area of Overton Down, after a few seasons of increasingly inconvenient cultivation, was put down to pasture. The Barbury estate had plenty of arable nearer to the centre on the northern Marlborough Downs, and its southern peripheral area was most appropriately used for unenclosed grazing. Sheep and cattle on Fyfield and Overton Downs henceforth munched their way through the centuries, creating the downland sward so valued 2500 years later. In the last centuries BC, they could well have been joined by horses, trained for racing and the chase, no doubt, but also, perhaps, quietly for more combative purposes.

For five centuries, the local scene remained essentially unchanged. A few of the new, fashionable iron objects began to circulate, but a real problem was that you had to have specialist smithing equipment — at least an anvil, heavy hammer and tongs — before you could make any tools for the farm. Then, too, the material was difficult to work and tended to produce heavy, blunt tools and somewhat unglamorous ornaments. What price your status if you give someone a brooch which then turns rusty?

Iron seemed to have little future, and bronze remained best. Of course there were alarms and excursions but for most of the time, and without major interruptions, people farmed the local resources in the sense that they looked after them while using them to maintain their way of life. Land-use was fairly intense, but the lessons of over-intensity had been learnt. Erosion was controlled because it was known about. Most of the local downs were grass, summer pastures among the banks and lynchets of derelict arable fields;

where husbandry was practised, run-off was contained in enclosed fields in which the soils were fed with manure and the rotation of crops was carefully managed. Different parts of the woodland were also carefully managed for different purposes. Coppicing was widely practised, for example, and the source of much of the wood needed for hurdles and fuel in a landscape now largely bereft of standing timber. The need for intensified land-use was lessened somewhat when the political powers of the 'hill-fort lords' declined; indeed, it was only from Martinsell and the settlement growing along the scarp-top outside the redundant defences that demands for supplies and services continued to come. Most of Fyfield and Overton were, in practice, free of such burdens, and had become largely self-sufficient in a reasonably sustainable relationship with their resources.

One such resource was the combination of circumstances — clay, fuel and water — to make pottery. This became a speciality, not apparently in Fyfield itself but a few miles to the east. Near the end of this period, a potter and his family arrived one day and set to work on the edge of the wood on the south bank of the Kennet near Marlborough. He soon had for sale some extraordinary pots, tall, smoothed and made on a wheel — and, though expensive, infinitely superior to the gritty, hand-made stuff with which most people still made do about the house. A small-scale industry developed and an extensive, semi-defended settlement sprawled along the edge of Savernake Forest, something of a frontier town dealing in trade and commerce conceptually as well as tenurially outside the local, politically-based territories of the now somewhat anachronistic hill-fort war-lords. People living westwards along the upper Kennet valley noted this and were well aware of its implications. Then one day, a troop of fearsome-looking warriors came clattering through, demanded the head-man's appearance and told him that all hereabouts were subject to (strange words) the 'Atrebates of Calleva'. Their effect was, however, significantly reduced when, a month later, another even more fearsome-looking troop came grandly by announcing that everything hereabouts belonged to the 'Dobunni of Corinium'. Wise old heads recognised that these incidents were merely the vapid gesturings of distant politicians and that, in fact, there was little to worry about. But next time it was different, seriously different.

THE PENULTIMATE BRITISH PHASE: THE ROMAN PERIOD

There was no mistaking the Romans when they marched in. Not that there was much fighting, though they killed a few men who happened to be standing in their way. Some thought that was from nervousness rather than bravado. They established a camp east of Fyfield, across the River Kennet from the potteries and the small town which had grown up along the northern edge of Savernake; and before many years had passed, their fortifications came to be called 'Cunetio' in a Latin version of the river name. Even faster was their cavalry out among the villagers along the upper Kennet valley, dragging off some of the strongest men to build their first fort very quickly in that summer of AD 45. But that was only the beginning. Forced labour now became the daily work of all the local males over 16 as these heavily armed men who had come from the east made mysterious marks on the ground and ordered their slaves — for that is what the peasantry had become — to build roads.

A swathe of land was cleared and levelled and built on all along the upper Kennet valley, first across the river south of the fort, then west along its southern bank until it had to re-cross the river, this time at Fyfield on a strange new thing called *'pons'*. The road was

67 Roman road between Fyfield and North Farm, along the north bank of the River Kennet, under the trees left centre. The road, hitherto suspected but unproven on this line, shows up as a white streak in the grass, actually a parch-mark produced in the hot, dry August of 1996. Immediately beyond the trees in the centre, the turnpike and modern A4 merge with it, apparently following it as it kinks left and westward on a causeway which has to be considered as possibly Roman. In the context here, the road is interpreted as one of the most significant elements to have been placed in the landscape of Fyfield and Overton, and is used to symbolise the very long-term and complex relationship between people living in this area and people moving through it — north–south as well as east–west.

engineered up out of the valley in a shallow cutting and down the other side; and then, where men sweated and cursed for two whole years, and some died in the mud, it was carried across the soggy marsh of an old ox-bow river channel on a causeway of stone to the dry land of the next hill-slope (**67**). No wonder few stones now lie along the riverside: they were heaved and shoved into 600m of causeway in one of Britain's earliest examples of road engineering. So impressive was that causeway that, quite unnecessarily in structural terms, the road continued on a 6ft-high (2m) *agger* up on to Overton Down until the moment it glimpsed the top of Silbury Hill. Then it adjusted its line to head straight towards that great relict of antiquity. And so came to pass one of the greatest single events in the history of Fyfield and Overton, an event which was to condition its landscape for the next 2000 years.

But the road-building programme — another road was built north from the fort up the valley of the Og — was but a part of a grander scheme. Once more, indeed for the third time, outsiders tried to impose a great landscape pattern on the area. This time, however, it was solely for material and fiscal gain. The military were immediately followed by the surveyors — the *agrimensores* — and the land-managers, both but the advance guard of the administrators and tax-collectors. The area had to pay for itself; indeed, it had to produce a profit, first to justify the invasion, second to pay for the expenses of bureaucracy, and thirdly to become taxable. So everywhere was, well within a couple of decades, re-designed, re-organised and generally turned around in order to become efficient in economic, not necessarily agrarian, terms.

Four things happened to the countryside, and all were consequential in a direct sense on the building of the road. They were the laying out of new field systems, a programme to convert marginal land into arable, the planting out of small communities into these 'new landscapes' to farm them, and the creation of estates with resident land-managers to oversee the whole operation from estate centres.

The road itself had been at first a military way, designed primarily as a reliable supply-line to the western frontier during the conquest period; and of course, long after the frontier had moved well away to west and north, it continued to be an official clear-way for imperial traffic even though it came increasingly to be used 'unofficially' by domestic and local traffic. The road to and from Bath became indeed a popular one, despite its single carriageway and the frustrations of being stuck behind a cart-load of Savernake timber going west or a wagon lumbering up from Mendip with a load of lead pigs. The developing world passed through Fyfield and Fyfield saw the new world pass through.

On the ground, the road was used as the axis for creating a sweep of new field systems: an extensive rectilinear landscape, for example, was laid out from Overton Hill and far to the north across Overton and Avebury Downs (**30**). It completely ignored, and indeed blocked, the track northwards along the ridgetop which had come to be used during the grassland phase of the last pre-Roman centuries; though a nod was made towards its former line by a short row, also at right angles to the road, of three wooden tombs. They stood among the fields as curiosities to the locals, until they rotted and were covered over; but their low mounds were always thereafter respected, until the 1960s.

Marginal land was also brought into cultivation, high on the downs on the clay-with-flints of Dillion Down and even in West Woods. There, instead of replanting trees after timber-felling, cultivation for cereals was attempted for a while. Indeed, every little bit of land was ploughed up in the decades around AD 100 if it was apparently unused and a potential cereal plot. And into this increasingly exploited landscape, people were planted out among the fields, up on Fyfield and Overton Downs and along the forest edges, in farmsteads and hamlets. A bolder step was taken beside the old traditional settlement place at Down Barn in Piggledean. There, on a pleasant south-facing slope above the dry combe, a large new village was laid out geometrically at the junction of old track and new road. The attraction placed by the authorities in trying to tempt farm-workers and their families here was a new, stone-footed cottage and a large garden for each settler, tax-free for five years. The opportunity was quickly taken up, by young couples in particular, and for a century the place was the centre of downland agrarian life (**37, 39**).

The practical needs of this intensive, State-driven arable farming, and incidentally of the farmworkers, was met by connecting the whole up with a network of country lanes. Some were new, built around the new fields, some were tracks from earlier times, and some were new lengths using or respecting old features in the landscape. Though some of the older farmers muttered about the regimentation of the countryside, and everyone was regretting the demands of the cereal tax, it was nevertheless a remarkably convenient thing about this new landscape that a cart could be driven along a continuous made-up track from Overton Down via Dillion and Fyfield Downs to Down Barn, Piggledean and the valley.

There, by the river, things were also changing, and always within the official imperative to make the countryside more tax-efficient. Alterations to the Kennet necessitated by the construction of the road causeway were extended, so that it not only ran straighter but had the effect of creating well-drained meadow and pasture beside it. For this, much of the rest of the valley bottom was cleared of sarsens too, and a good stone ford was constructed at Overton. There was talk of a corn-mill, but it was never actually built. At Fyfield, however, on the little knoll above where the river swerved to the north, a farm quickly developed as the estate centre. It was conveniently placed just north off the main road, incorporating a cluster of farm buildings around the west and north sides of an ever-grander domestic range facing south across the valley towards the distant woods (**35**). A largish farm developed in the similar position at (East) Overton too, but it was never owned by someone with enough money to equip it with central heating or beautify it with mosaics. Again, however, the real estate centre lay, as at Fyfield, just north of the main road, with a rather unsightly village straggling down the slope between it and the road. But even that did not develop into a grand country house (**36**).

With so much of the area's agricultural wealth disappearing in tax demands each year, estate and domestic grandeur could only follow the arrival of someone with outside resources; and such people naturally tended to invest their wealth further west along the road, in the environs of Bath or on the fashionable Cotswolds. The early Roman exploitation of the Fyfield/Overton area masked its basic agrarian richness through taxation; but its true character remained, and its time would come again when the heavy hand of State bureaucracy weakened. Farming meanwhile continued hereabouts, and indeed flourished under central direction in what was generally a prosperous area lying between Mildenhall (*Cunetio*) and its nearby pottery kilns to the east and the villas of the southern Cotswolds centred on Bath.

In the fourth century AD, however, long-term change was quickening. There were still lots of people around in the countryside but unease was in the air, rumours abounded and the old sense of security seemed to have evaporated. Many of the families prominent in rural affairs now spent much of their time in towns; some had moved completely to places where great curtain walls were now being built around increasingly introspective urban communities. The military, and state officials, were seen less frequently, which was good in one sense, but who was policing the countryside? Tangible wealth in the great houses began to be less noticeable; there were stories about mysterious wagon-loads disappearing into the night and even of treasures being buried.

Much of the arable on the Downs fell out of cultivation, the land there reverting to use by the more mobile 'crops' of sheep and cattle. Some families saw the opportunity to break out of their servile position in a now-crumbling hierarchy and set up a new farm of timber buildings on unwanted land among the outlines of the former arable fields on Overton Down (**40**). The permanent arable was kept going lower down and along the valley, but cereal growing was now for local use, not export; and the labourers increasingly found they were left to their own devices rather than having to work to order and for the benefit of landlord and tax-collector.

Strangers — dispossessed tenant farmers from further east, they said — increasingly straggled along a road which by the end of the fourth century was falling badly into disrepair. There were others too from time to time, men on horses, armed with iron swords and spears but wearing no tunic and no armour. They arrived across the downland ways or along the forest trails, bringing neither threats nor gifts. They simply ignored the villagers as they looked with curiosity and apparently appraised the place, speaking neither Latin nor British yet muttering with guttural sounds to each other.

Travellers brought stories of such strangers arriving by the hundred from boats along the eastern shores and up the river valleys; and of their ruthless behaviour when they met anyone who would accost them. Even the unadventurous farmer-workers of Fyfield and Overton realised that the Roman order was breaking down and some regretted the loss of security. Others took land and their freedom, setting up new farms on old lands now without owners. The villa at Fyfield was no longer inhabited and its fabric gently subsided into a ruin; but one room on its south side was maintained, its roof at least rain-proof, and some people met there each week to pray to yet another foreign god but one at least who offered some sort of hope even in death. The villa by the road in Overton, however, was vandalised once it was realised that its absentee owners were not going to come back and could not do much about it even if they did. Outsiders took tiles and building stone away by the cart-load to re-use elsewhere; the locals, with memories and more diffidently, took souvenirs, imagining as they placed a patch of lifted tiles on their trampled earth floor what it would have been like to have a real floor of baked clay tiles.

At the Overton Down settlement, they 'played' at windows and central heating with bits of glass and hypocaust, but were sufficiently well-off now farming part of the villa estate to their own profit. They were able to buy real glass vessels for their table and beads for decoration, though their table-ware was now becoming unreplaceable and cash seemed to be worth very little. It was important to have dried grain and fair cuts of meat to exchange for goods, but even so it was becoming increasingly difficult, despite proper observances to several deities, to sustain a viable sort of self-sufficiency on the downs (**40**).

It never seemed to become really light nowadays, not at least with that bright sunlight of a frosty March morning or a July afternoon after a heavy shower; the winters seemed longer, the days duller and summers not really hot any more. The cereal crops did not quite ripen however long into September they were left standing; the grass was not long enough for hay-making in June like it used to be in the old days; and the sheep had nibbled the grass down to nothingness by July. It was difficult — and just a little eerie, like the end of the world in slow motion. A carter struggling along the pot-holed road with a load of used Cotswold roofing tiles from Bath said he had met someone who had met a sailor from the northern seas who spoke of giant whales spouting smoke and fumes into the skies before disappearing. One sad day about AD 540, with illness among them and strangers camped nearby on the Ridgeway skyline, the Overton Down people moved out, ending over nearly 3000 years of habitation around Down Barn.

THE LAST BRITISH PHASE

Curiously, there then followed neither total collapse nor complete take-over, but a brief period of tremendous activity. The weather quickly recovered but a new threat became apparent, one with which Fyfield and Overton were not unfamiliar: the strangers on the Ridgeway were not alone. The local communities from *Aquae Sulis* to *Cunetio* for once acted together, agreed on a joint leader with full powers to act, and set about one of the largest construction jobs ever undertaken in the district. Monumentally, it was on a scale of the same order as that of Avebury henge monment, Silbury Hill, Martinsell hill-fort and the Roman road through the Kennet valley. A great rampart with a ditch along its northern edge was built right across country from north of Devizes to near Shalbourne in east Wiltshire. Everybody who could turned out that summer and on through the winter to dig and heap 'their' bit, for rumours of warriors massing to the north were rife (**55–6, colour plate 5, 27**).

The great frontier line was built within a year and, even though it was incomplete in Overton, everyone prepared to move to its south if need be. Most of the lands of Fyfield and Overton lay briefly empty, as the inhabitants feared the worst, but no great attack transpired. Instead, the newcomers arrived in dribs and drabs, their leaders armed admittedly but actually at the head of landless farmers looking for farm-sites where they could work for their livelihood. The great earthwork, where so many had laboured so frantically, was left lying like a useless hulk stretched out along the landscape; it soon began to weather and slump on the downlands and become shrub-covered in Savernake. The locals returned to their farms and, while some of the incomers moved on through, others stopped and began to re-cultivate and graze on patches of the now-abundant marginal land.

In truth, the uselessness of the last great British line of defence marked the end of the Old World. Two and a half thousand years of farming and living in a British landscape began to change into something different, living and farming in an English countryside. Symbolic of the change was that after a few decades the newcomers, knowing nothing of why or when the great ditched rampart had been built but recognising its existence, attributed its origin to the power of their father god, hence Woden's *dic*. One of the new farmers who staked out a claim on uninhabited land built his steading south of Wansdyke beyond Savernake, on the fringes of the old estate; he later acquired grazing rights far to the north on Lockeridge Down. His name was Aethelferth, the first known Englishman of Overton (**17a**, **63**).

13

And along to Lettice

Most of the downland lay uninhabited between AD 500–1000 but it continued to be used in various ways, mostly for sheep-grazing. One group of Saxons, arriving across the downs from the north, tried living on the deserted high land and indeed began another phase of use at Down Barn by building a new animal fold for the herd and flock they brought with them. They dug it on relatively sheltered land beside — actually partly on — the   traditional path up the dene from valley to the high downland (**31**). This group was part of a larger, loosely related community, not always easy neighbours either to each other or to the local Britons.

The leader of the new West Overton group established his headquarters on the old, traditional 'Headlands' site, close to the eastern boundary of the territory he wanted to claim. He built rectangular halls close to the nettle-heaps and elderberry trees of the dimly remembered villa-site and, so the stories said, the dwelling place of the ancestral chieftains long before the hated Romans crossed the seas (**36**). He was clearly seeking a validation for his territorial claims, hoping too that the aura of the ancient site would afford some sort of protection to his small number of followers. They stayed long enough for their aged ones to die and they buried them with their own alien ceremonial in an old mound up on the ridgetop which they had followed from the riverlands of *Thamesis*.

But these were the temporary arrangements of newcomers unsure of themselves and the resources they would colonise. The future lay off the exhausted downs and it lay with others. In the years around AD 550 the local scene was changed politically as, with little warning, an army looking for conquest and power moved into and through the area, not from the north but from the south. Wansdyke would have been facing the wrong way had the locals had the wit to man it! Nevertheless, the army had a use for it, as a line to fall back on should they be forced to retreat from the north; so they left two detachments to guard the gates, under commanders respectively called Titferth and Edgar (**63**).

Basically, the way of life continued: farming, silviculture, hunting, fishing; but now all the inhabitants were subject to West Saxon lords who very obviously managed their newly redefined estates by direct control and with constant reference to 'royal laws' which everyone, without knowing what they were, was required to obey. By around AD 600, the focus of habitation had shifted emphatically and permanently into the valley. Power was lodged there again also but, unlike the habitations, it was not to stay there for ever. Four main 'village' settlements grew up along the valley: Fyfield, Lockeridge (where Lockeridge House now is), East Overton and West Overton, with (Lockeridge) Dene set back half-a-mile (1km) behind a ridge to the south. Clatford and Manton lay immediately downstream, and East and West Kennet just to the west across what was emerging as the main track of the north–south downland route. Each village was the centre-place of a long narrow estate, reflecting earlier arrangements and indeed deliberately picking out ancestral places, like burial mounds and standing stones, to link the present with the Old Ones and to gain respect for the now formalised boundaries (**55**).

The limits of these agreed territories were inspected every year by the community leaders to each side. This was very important, not just to ensure that neighbours were not encroaching but also to reinforce the idea that each community had its own identity as well as its own territory. The annual Walk of the Ealdormen-Jury was a solemn event, critically followed by most of the land-workers on both sides of the boundary determined both to cede not an inch yet to gain official recognition of that extra furrow they accidentally slipped on to the edge of their strip of land (**63**).

This whole idea of formal estates had been reinforced about AD 630 when a man with a small band of followers arrived, saying he was from the king and a new and greater King, the King of all kings and all the West Saxons and the peoples beyond. He carried not a spear or a sword but crossed sticks, and yet he spoke of war and peace. The man stood on the little knoll overlooking the river at Fyfield, and he preached to a small group of believers in the same sort of God who met secretly in the now roofless 'holy room' of the ruinous villa. He stood on the little knoll overlooking the same river at Overton, and he preached. And he stood near the ford where the way off the downs crossed that same river Kennet, and he preached there too.

Most ignored him and his ridiculous claims but a few took up his Word and came to speak of this great King at the same places. They were marked by wooden crosses; and then others met there too, regularly, and within two generations the communities of Fyfield, Overton and Kennet were Christian in practice as well as in name. By the late seventh century, they worshipped their Lord in new wooden buildings called churches, put up where the missionary had preached, the first overtly religious buildings as distinct from open structures to appear in this landscape for 2500 years. In them, in the presence of their invisible and demanding Lord (just like their earthly one, as some silently noted), the local people had thoughts of a better life to come as, for the first time in centuries, hope became a genuine factor in daily life.

Nevertheless, in that real life, these new Christian communities worked for their earthly lord and themselves, just like their predecessors. Now they were very conscious that their working life was carried out within the boundaries of an estate, each of which had to be at one and the same time self-sufficient and the producer of a surplus. Most of the surplus went to the lord as free labour and as 'rent' but increasingly this new religion and its priests took produce too. Such was the price of eternal salvation.

The church belonged to a particular place, giving it a focal point and an identity: the people of Fyfield knew they were different from East Overtonians. Yet the Church took away from that place too. This became particularly marked when the two estates of Overton not only came to be owned by the Church but passed to different and rival establishments. Fyfield and East Overton became part of the great estates of the powerful Bishop of Winchester while West Overton passed to the Abbess of Wilton. These legalities were far more important locally in the eleventh century than the big event nationally when King William and his knights seized political power in the kingdom in 1066.

Long before then, the framework controlling the overall pattern of life and the daily lives, in Fyfield and Overton, had been set, and this basic, dual ownership conditioned matters for more than half a millennium. More immediately, the Bishop began laying out a 'new town' or burgh beside the church at East Overton as the centre of his new estates in Kennet, and he refurbished the old church so that it graced the east end of the new main street on the highest point (**48**, **50**, **colour plate 1**). He caused drainage works to be undertaken on the flood plain south of Fyfield church and encouraged people to inhabit that area too. The old settlement at Dene was also re-organised so that it better befitted its position on the old King's road and on the main link between the new and old parts of the Episcopal estate respectively on the Kennet and in the Vale of Pewsey. In contrast, the old settlement of West Overton, hard along the through-track that was coming to be known as the 'People's Path', and despite possessing its own church, drifted into desertion under its new management. People tended to move across to the other side of the estate and live near to the new East Overton and the ford on the boundary between them.

Change was in the tenth-century air and other developments before 1066 saw, once again, villagers tackling marginal land. A dry valley up through the East Overton woods where some wild horses once ran was cleared and it came to be known as *hyrsleage*, 'mare's clearing' (**56**). Some downland in Fyfield was ploughed up and disconcertingly found to have heavy clay-with-flints overlying the chalk. A shelter for the farmer was built and some large pits were dug to get at the chalk so that the clay plough-soil could be marled, but the experiment was not a success and the area was soon abandoned to scrub. Two hundred years later, the disturbance was marked by a patch of deciduous woodland. The area was called Raddun, 'Red Down', after the colour of the freshly-turned plough-soil. On the edges of the great royal forest of Savernake, five wooden cottages were erected for the woodsman, huntsman, carpenter, trapper and forest warden.

The Normans rode through from Marlborough, where a new castle was built on a prehistoric mound, but they did not stay long in Fyfield or Overton, for these newcomers had no stake in this land. The coming of new lordships in many other places was marked by the construction of new churches; so, as much for the sake of status in the eyes of his fellow-men as of his Lord, the Bishop of Winchester as lord of the two manors of Overton and Fyfield rebuilt their pre-Norman churches about AD 1100. One extended with its graveyard over the Fyfield Roman villa and the other, also with its graveyard, took in some ground formerly occupied by the early settlers. The third Anglo-Saxon church, nominally in West Overton, had already been forgotten and successors of its former worshippers now went to one or other of the renewed stone churches in East Overton or East Kennet.

Ecclesiastical and tenurial complexity was further complicated by the arrival in the mid-twelfth century of yet another major religious landlord who created a new estate in an already crowded landscape. This time it was the Knights Templar, a body whose reputation for godliness and valour had been flourished even along the Kennet valley but whose intrusion at Lockeridge as yet another absentee landlord was deeply suspect. Before long, suspicion was confirmed as a seigneurial attempt was made to impose more rigorous terms of tenure upon tenants long-accustomed to unwritten, traditional ways of going about things in these parts. Resentment was such that the tenants resisted in a quite extraordinary demonstration of popular strength in unity, while the rest of the valley, landlord and peasant alike, held its breath to see what happened as the very fabric of medieval rural life was challenged. In fact, the dispute dragged on for decades and was never properly resolved at law; in practice, the tenants grudgingly and tacitly ceded some points, for they had their lives to live and families to feed, but the Templars failed overall to impose their new style of exploitative management. They left their marks on the landscape, nevertheless, with a new, planned village where Lockeridge stands today, a large abandoned earthwork enclosure up on the downs at Wick, and small-scale but extensive assarting in West Woods perpetuated in clearings and place-names still there today (**46b, 55**).

The twelfth and thirteenth centuries were among the most successful of all centuries in the area. Locally there was peace, no major setbacks, the weather was generally good and seemed to be improving, farming was expanding as the local communities became larger from generation to generation, and the hard grind of agrarian life was slowly ameliorated. Domestic chores, for example, were made a little easier by even a labourer being able to afford to buy a few of the locally wheel-made pottery jars and platters at Marlborough market; the estate blacksmith provided horseshoes and nails; iron knives

68 Thirteenth-century sheep-shears, Raddun: symbolic of the long-term significance of sheep-farming to this landscape.

and a few tools could be bought from the travelling salesman who might also have trinkets in bronze, tin and glass. And for the better-off, there was glazed pottery brought across the Plain from Clarendon and imported goods such as glass and wine from France. Perhaps the biggest improvement for many was, however, a proper house, still earth-floored, timber-framed and thatched but at least founded on properly-laid sarsen walls (**43, colour plate 23**).

Beyond, the surrounding landscape was slowly but continually being improved. The big open fields which had developed in the preceding centuries continued to be intensively cultivated on both sides of the river, except in West Overton where the manorial lands, reflecting ancient arrangements, did not contain large acreages of downland pasture. The small area north of the Kennet was therefore kept for sheep, forcing all the arable on to the slopes south of the river (**2, 58, 70, colour plate 2**). All three fields of the open field system were, as a result, south west of the village, forming a single, huge expanse of unhedged, treeless landscape which is still there today. There, and in the other manors' open fields, matters were arranged in a highly disciplined way under the direction of the reeves. Access to the fields and their furlongs, by year, by season and for different purposes, was strictly regulated; yet, within them, strip-holders were making personal arrangements with friends and consolidating their holdings as a matter of convenience. Lengths of fencing, even the occasional hedge, were beginning to appear, as personal parcels of land were defined. In the valley below, the bottomlands were now thoroughly organised into meadow and pasture, with the water carefully controlled to flood the grass at the right time and to provide power to the corn-mills at the two Overtons and Fyfield.

Yet again, however, it was beyond the permanent arable that the main landscape changes were occurring. Two new frontier settlements in terms of their estate positions were so poised on the margins that, although they were not to know it then, both were to fail. High on the northern downs and close to a patch of woodland, a new settlement developed on Red Down. It began earlier as a shepherd's place for overnight stays during lambing, and was then lived in temporarily during the summer while the flocks grazed the vast areas of inter-commoned pastures. One Richard moved up there in the 1220s with the encouragement of the estate; he came to be known as 'Richard of Raddun'. He was helped to build a stone-based house for his family, sharing it with the oxen he looked after for the ploughing which once more spread out across Fyfield Down (**41–2, 44**). For 60 years, first his son and then his grandson farmed successfully there, performing their duties (more or less) as specified by the estate; and the family enjoyed a modest prosperity. Their farmhouse became a farmstead, with specialist buildings for the oxen, horses, cattle and sheep (**colour plate 23**). They enclosed it, again with help from the estate; and kept it in good repair. Shaw, *Schaga* in 1165, was in contrast far to the south and a much larger settlement, revived as a new, planned village with a church on an ancient site south of old Woden's ditch; but it was cursed from the start, perhaps by the ancient god's magic, cold in the wind on its hill-top and with cold soils full of clay. It had died before 1400 (**55, 59**).

During its heyday, however, the Savernake woods were being exploited as never before. In the twelfth, thirteenth and fourteenth centuries, individual pioneers sought to make a livelihood outside the communal arable by trying to found a home and create some new fields hacked out of the Forest and heathland. One was St Quintyn in the twelfth century; another was Ralph atte Hethe in the later fourteenth. Each estate had its own share of this great resource and the tenants had been letting their animals forage in them for centuries, just as they had been collecting fallen wood, coppicing oak and hazel, and picking the medicinal plants and edible fungi. Now, however, in this period of unprecedented economic growth, timber was in great demand and land was at a premium. Young farming families, with few opportunities on the old land, began moving right up to the woodland edge, even into the ancient forest, to cut and hack and root up trees so their cereal crops could gain a foothold. These early pioneers lived in isolated cottages at Breach, Fosbury and Boreham (**55, 57**).

Equally, those who owned the forest and had jurisdiction over how it was exploited and by whom, were increasingly worried about the relentless encroachments and blatant disregard for ancient Forest Law. Those locals who ignored their warnings, and there seemed to be more of them each year, were brought before the Forest Court, or *eyres*, and fined. But the clandestine hunting, wood cutting, grazing, felling, grubbing up and ploughing continued, involving the supposedly good but actually notorious nuns of Wilton Abbey. Even the pits, fences and deep ditches alongside earthen banks which the forest wardens had constructed around each wood to regulate the movement of people and animals had little effect.

But something was going wrong beyond the control of individual farmers, however good. In one disastrous decade at the start of the fourteenth century, the Templars were sequestrated and, as the prosperous economy began to change, trade waned and fewer travellers appeared. Worst of all, however, the weather was deteriorating and quite suddenly the marginality of places like Raddun and Fosbury became a critical factor. A run of bad harvests culminated in the two wet years of 1316 and 1317, and the farmsteads were abandoned in 1318 once it was apparent that, for the third year running, there was to be no harvest. Other upland farms were deserted in the early fourteenth century too. The sheep and the shepherds continued to use the downs as vast pastures, of course, but no-one lived there any more. The new period of retreat itself continued throughout the fourteenth century. Many of the villagers died around 1350 in the numerous years of plague, fewer children were born or matured and land was left to the weeds. Indeed, by 1400 the local population was only a half of what it had been in 1300 and, once more, signs of abandonment were everywhere in the landscape.

At East Overton and Fyfield, both villages drew back in extent towards the two churches; West Overton shrank to the size of a farmstead and a few cottages; Dene and Lockeridge were semi-deserted, and neither ever recovered. But in a sense, recession played to the area's real strength which is its extensive pasture, not its arable; and despite the obvious signs of retrenchment compared to the expansive years of the twelfth and thirteenth centuries, sheep farming not only continued but flourished throughout the fourteenth century and into modern times. It brought relative wealth to the lords of the manor at a time when elsewhere their counterparts were forcing people to leave the land to convert it to sheep-runs where formerly it had been arable. Winchester and Wilton, through trade inland and abroad, did very well on the backs of the Fyfield and Overton sheep; and so, to a degree, did the locals who survived in a form of farming which does not require large numbers of workers.

Indeed, some local families began buying up farm leases across the downs and soon controlled enough land to compete with the largest of the regional players. Winchester and Wilton recognised this new breed of successful farmer and soon, as long as the rents and payments in kind continued, they withdrew more and more from daily estate management. In such a situation, indeed with an uneasy national situation, many of the landed locals acted as freely as they wished. Deer hunting became a common pastime, especially enjoyed by the Wroughton family of East Overton, who, for example, were charged in 1490 with hunting 'out of those wodes of Chychangles and Chichangles Peketheket … a Bukke a doo and a preket (a doe of the second year) with greyhounds and bowes and arowes slewe without lycence'.

The area was certainly well-worth having when, as suddenly as previous changes, the whole land was once more claimed by an outsider — this time the king — and, apart from Upper Lockeridge, re-apportioned to a secular landlord. From the middle of the sixteenth century it was the Earls of Pembroke who were the absentee landlords instead of an Abbess in Wilton and a Prior in Winchester. It did not make all that much difference to the workers of the land (**69**).

The Earls appointed their own men to manage the affairs of the villages. The manor of West Overton was leased to Richard Frankelyn, whilst Richard Kingsmill moved into East Overton, which still included Fyfield. Upper Lockeridge manor was first given to Anne of Cleves as part of her marriage arrangement, but after only six months she and Henry were divorced and the land passed to Thomas Goddard. These new men brought new ideas. Large, rectangular sheepfolds were constructed on the downs (**46a**), as were deer parks, so fashionable at the time. One park was enclosed on Hackpen Down by the old chalk track; another was fenced in through the woods at the south end of Clatford (**37, 55**). Much of the old woodland which had been over-exploited in the previous centuries was grubbed up and replanted with oak, willow, maple and hazel saplings, and down on the river bed, osier beds appeared to produce the thin, pliable withies the basket and hurdle-makers required (**48**). The movement of beasts across the Pembroke estates was also reviewed; firm dates and times were now set out so the land could be grazed, and simultaneously manured, when appropriate and where required. More hedges and fences appeared, not only to keep the animals off the crops, but also because the manorial farmers wanted to consolidate their arable into small fields. Meanwhile, the peasants continued their daily toil, the millstone turned and the villages slipped into becoming part of the Wiltshire rural scene, pleasant but unremarkable.

The years came and went, as did lords and villagers alike. In the outside world England was spreading its net across the globe, yet in the Kennet valley little stirred. Admittedly

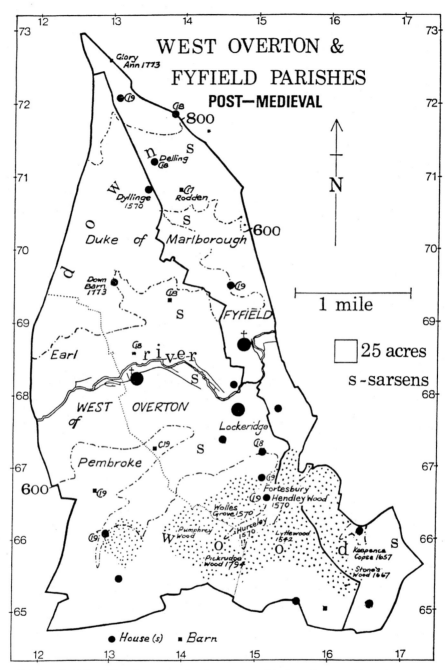

69 *Map of Fyfield and West Overton parishes showing some of the farms, houses and barns that occupied the landscape from the reign of Elizabeth I to the time of Lettice Sweetapple. Many of the names would have been those which characterised the landscape that Lettice knew. Though ownership and tenure of the land became very complex during these post-medieval centuries, basically the Earl of Pembroke held the historic manor of West Overton with Shaw, while the Duke of Marlborough held all the rest, including East Overton and Lockeridge which now constitute the greater part of the civil parish of West Overton.*

Key: *the five letters 'S' indicate the concentrations of sarsen stones.*

Lockeridge House, a fine red brick mansion, was built about 1700 and the properties of East Overton, Lockeridge and Fyfield passed to a new landlord, the Duke of Marlborough, in the 1750s. On the whole, though, changes in the landscape can easily go unnoticed. The slow steps towards the modern era were, however, being taken, even here in this quiet backwater of England.

Perhaps the most important aspect of the area's history during these years before Enclosure was the local industries. The systematic removal of the natural sandstones (sarsens) hereabouts expanded as demand for building stone grew apace. Common though the practice had been for centuries, the architects whose buildings were emerging from the ashes of the Great Fire of London demanded the finest-quality sarsen and soon the upper Kennet valley was loud with the noise of hammers on iron wedges and of carts rumbling, heavily-laden with shaped blocks along the road to Marlborough (**colour plate 9**).

High up on the downs and in the overgrown hollows of Wansdyke, the heavy, red clay which had so tired the medieval plough-teams, was being dug to produce bricks. Kilns appeared alongside the great clay pits and the villagers became accustomed on 'firing days' to the smoke plumes along both horizons. Not all the bricks and sarsens were carted away to the towns, of course. With such an abundance of local building materials and with the skills at hand, the villages were transformed. Old houses were given brick extensions, some even second floors, whilst many others had the ancient timber and clunch walls replaced by bricks.

While some villagers prospered, others sank, and just as it does to some in the late twentieth century, this phenomenon pained the Reverend Fowle of Fyfield. So, along the banks of the Kennet, five parish houses were built for the poorest members of the community. They were those who had fared worst from the very advances which were meant to make the labourer's task less arduous. Later landowners were less generous and these cottages, never the most substantial of buildings, quickly fell into disrepair once their aged inhabitants had passed on.

The new technologies of the age also made it possible for the power of the wind to be harnessed. On the spur of land which gave Lockeridge its name, a windmill was put up, while south of West Overton another was built among the strips of Lettice and the other land-holders. The age of experiment saw the waters of the Kennet diverted to flood the meadow-land more accurately than ever. The fords were repaved, but the locals and travellers now crossed the Kennet by footbridges. The London to Bath road along the valley was taken over by a private concern, one of the most significant things to happen locally for, as in Roman times, it allowed the produce out and, as significant, the outside world in.

The new turnpike was of course immediately fitted with fine milestones and a toll-house to collect the traveller's contributions towards its upkeep. Many, of course, dodged the toll-house by using the ancient track across the downs above Wroughton Copse, even if the journey was painfully bumpy. Dovecotes, barns, stables, inns and gamekeepers' lodges started appearing in the landscape too, and further south there was talk of a canal to link up the Bristol Avon with the Thames. So, by the end of the eighteenth century, on the eve of the Industrial Revolution and Enclosure, the villages of the Kennet valley had become rather busy, prosperous places, in local terms at least.

Lettice Sweetapple was now 72, an old woman whose uneventful personal life had co-incided with, but perhaps not been directly affected by, the accretion of large parts of the British Empire, the loss of the American colonies and the seemingly endless reign of a Hanoverian king increasingly beset with personal difficulties. What she could not avoid during her later life, however, was the speed and rapidity of major changes that she

*70 Landscape without trees, West Overton: a blank area which can be explained historically. The view is to the north across an unenclosed landscape, the northern part of West Overton manor (see **2**). In the foreground is part of the northernmost common field, Ditch Hedge Field. Then there is the Kennet. Left of the white track to the smoke is The Cow Down, always pasture; the smoke and bushes mark the site of a penning where sheep were folded and flocks and herds watered. Beyond, and to the right, was The Farm, an area used primarily as pasture but variously for arable too. None of this was ever Enclosed and hedged. To the left on historically unenclosed downland are the barrows on Overton Hill and, dramatic in an otherwise treeless landscape, the tree-clumps on Avebury Down near the Ridgeway. On the right is West Farm at the end of the village street and, beyond, the Bell Inn beside the turnpike (and A4) which cut through this open landscape and, by 1794, was hedged as far as the white track.*

both saw and directly experienced. The French Revolution and the Napoleonic Wars, the increasing size of towns and urban populations, national economic growth and a re-emerging empire — these and other major events and trends rumbled away somewhere off-stage beyond her metropolis, Marlborough; but there was also an air of disruption and drama enough in Fyfield and Overton parishes around AD 1800.

People longed for 'the good old days' when you knew who was who, the children showed respect and a gentleman was a gentleman. Now, there were new people in the big houses, and if the big houses were bespoke, then they built themselves new ones out in the fields. It was all change — in the people, the houses, the comings and goings, and in the very fields themselves. And everything seemed to be judged by money alone. Tenants lost their rights in the face of influence and unrepeatable offers for their holdings, and the big open spaces of the common fields became, except in West Overton, nasty private little hedged fields, no good for gleaners and no good for skylarks. The beginning of the nineteenth century heralded a new book in the long, long history of the land of Lettice Sweetapple, a land she left in 1805.

EPILOGUE:

Lettice Sweetapple in imagination

There was nothing unusual about Lettice Sweetapple except possibly her name.

She lived just over 200 years ago in a small village called West Overton in Wiltshire. Her roomy house, inherited from her parents, with its sarsen stone walls and thatched roof, lay lengthways on the main street, its two front windows facing directly across the pot-holed track to the ancient manor house, now the home of Edward Pumphrey. The village stocks, with their well-worn holes, stood on a muddy patch outside the walls enclosing the manor house and farm. Well-fenced paddocks and a neat, well-kept orchard lay behind and to the sides.

Each day, off the street through the gate she was forever repairing, Lettice brought her five, contented cows. Once in the yard, they needed no cajoling, for they knew their routine better than she. When it rained, they lurched across the cobbles, always deep in muck, to the byre set on a slight slope a little down from the house. In fine weather, however, the beasts stood patiently in the yard, waiting while Lettice sat neatly on her three-legged stool and set about milking them. Her hens clucked as if approvingly, busy scratching in the dust under the beady eye of a slightly aloof cockerel.

Her two pigs had a sty behind the house with a scruffy bit of earth to lie in. It was time, Lettice thought, for them to be moved again. They only travelled a few yards (from the commotion one would have thought it a mile!), and soon they would begin their rooting and snuffling again on a fresh patch; but it meant asking one of the village men in to help her make the pen secure in its new position, and she hated asking favours. 'But you must,' she told herself, for the ground the pigs moved off never needed much digging and she enjoyed planting it up quickly to produce the most wonderful vegetables, especially lettuces.

Her main garden and orchard were further away from the house, leading towards the back lane. The plot was only small, but it was enough for a single woman and she was able to keep herself in the basics of her daily dinner at noon, potatoes, onions and beans, usually in a soup flavoured with garden and wild herbs and perhaps with a taste of the rabbit that the gamekeeper occasionally left on her back doorstep after dark. She hated cabbages and, unlike most cottages in the village, her home did not smell of them. Sometimes, as a treat for afterwards, she ate plums, or had them for supper with her damson jam or crab-apple jelly on her gritty, home-made bread. She had always liked apples and managed to harvest enough from her orchard in most years to have one every day. With her daily milk, fresh eggs and weekly treats of her own salted pork, she lived quite well by villagers' standards, always busy, as they remarked, though sharing her loneliness with none. Her pride and joy were her flowers, planted and coaxed and tended and pricked on beds she had made herself, always a flash of rare summer and autumnal colour in a rather drab little village at a time when every family croft had to earn its keep with cabbages, pigs and potatoes.

Her neighbour, John Cook, was a kind, honest man. His family had been in the village for generations, and not so long ago actually lived in the manor house. Even now Jane Cook and John the younger held all the land along the road which led south, out of the village, to Hookland. Mrs Martin was her other neighbour, living in the first house you come to in West Overton when travelling in along Kennet Drove from the Ridgeway. Mrs Martin's place was neat and its vegetable garden was always well-tended, partly because Mrs Martin believed, she would whisper to Lettice, that she ought to make an effort seeing as her place was the sight that greeted visitors to the village and you never knew who might step by.

Mrs Martin would answer to no other name than 'Mrs Martin', though everyone else was called by their Christian name, apart from Mr Pumphrey of course and Robert Scaplehorne, who was called 'Scaps'. Lettice knew Mrs Martin's name was 'Alexandra', and thought it a beautiful name, but she also knew that a very young wife had insisted on the formality of her married name since the day, a whole life-time ago, when the London-Bath stage-coach had dramatically pulled off the turnpike for the postman to leave a message at the manor house. It simply said that a William Martin of Overton had been killed at the Battle of Plassey. To John Cook the Elder fell the task of telling the expectant mother that her child would be fatherless; and within a day the mother-to-be was childless, for the baby was still-born in her trauma. It was one of those times, so Lettice heard tell, when the village badly missed not having a church.

Now in her sixties, Mrs Martin had never re-married and kept herself to herself. She no longer worked the plough as much as she used to, yet she still had a large amount of land in West Overton, including Upper and Lower Chichangles woods. Much of the work was done by local young men who had not yet secured their own tenancies. There were rumours about how they might have been recompensed in years gone by but now Mrs Martin, as prudent about her past as with her parsimonious Company pension, paid them in kind from the produce they farmed for her. She and Lettice were good neighbours and friends, but not *confidantes*.

Lettice was a tenant for life of the Earl of Pembroke, a status which gave her some local standing. Her considerable land holding was a family inheritance and, with her brother Thomas, she made sure it was well-farmed. Her land lay dispersed across the valley slopes and the southern hills. By the River Kennet, she held a good plot of meadow, called North Mead, which sat between the water-mill and the London Road. She also held Hill Ground and Long Ground, a couple of fertile fields full of long grass and daisies either side of Kennet Drove, much appreciated by her cows.

Her field crops were two cereals: mainly barley for the local breweries, which produced her small and variable cash income; and a little wheat for herself and some landless villagers to make their own bread. These crops were grown on the most precious part of her life-holding, some two dozen strips of land in the great common fields to the south. They were disposed across the thin, chalky soils of Double Hedge, Ditch Hedge and Windmill Fields. 'It's all very well talking about this equal shares for everyone,' the commoners complained, 'but it makes for a terribly inefficient way of producing crops in practice and in any case some do better than others because the land changes so much in quality across this great dome of chalk down.' Little did they know it but they were anticipating Enclosure before conceptualising it; as indeed was Lettice.

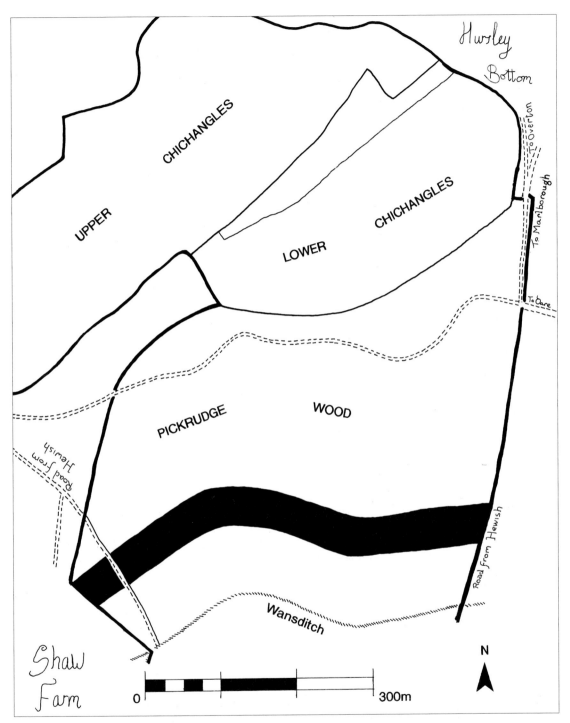

71 *Map of Pickrudge Wood and Chichangles in 1794, showing the land of Lettice Sweetapple (solid black), mirroring the curves of Wansdyke as built 1300 years previously. The rest of Pickrudge Wood was divided up into similar strips, all fallen out of cultivation by the end of the century. This detail is taken from Map D of the Map of the Manor of West Overton (see **2**).*

Partly to try to offset some of the perceived inequality, partly for ease of working, she had managed to exchange a few of her strips with her neighbours, and was now able to farm several small blocks of inter-connecting strips. This saved her time and effort and, therefore, cash, for she was not a full-time farmer and each year had to hire plant and equipment she had never felt justified in buying for herself. She had managed to adjust her holdings by the 1790s to the extent that she hoped to save herself two whole days of hire-charges. For one thing she could now farm her larger blocks by the Alton cross-roads by simply crossing Hollow Snap or, if she wished, work her five long, narrow belts of land down Double Hedge Furlong and into Sheepridge Furlong without lifting the plough. Such cost-efficient trimmings were important because, as she aged, she was tending now to pay a ploughman to go with the hired ox-team and tackle which she had previously always worked herself. She was also developing the practice of sharing the costs of such a hiring over several days with neighbours in the fields, so that whole blocks of land could be ploughed as one. Then afterwards, she and her partners re-marked out their separate stints for planting, wondering the while whether it did not make more sense to carry out the whole process as one, and not just the ploughing.

Over at Savernake Park, which locals agreed was once part of the great Royal Forest, Lettice had also been able to arrange her acres wisely. They sat in a square block up against the hedge which divided West Overton from Lockeridge and Oare Common. It was a sheltered spot and in good years the 15 acres or so produced a fair crop considering the soil. Thorpe Chamberlaine, 'Scaps', John Cook and Mrs Martin had also been in the arrangement and they too had land that was not all that difficult to work, though none of them fared more than average on what had until recently been heath.

Over to the west, by the old Huish road, some villagers also held strips in Pickrudge Wood (71). Some of the older inhabitants, though, insisted on calling it by its ancient name, *Chichangles Pekethicket*. They loved wrapping their soft, slow vowels round the unaccustomed sharpness of a name that often came out as 'Chick Changles', sometimes lazily shortened with an unlettered accuracy to 'Chick hanger' or 'hangings'. Lettice knew the thickets of undergrowth that grew there on the slope, for she had hidden there as a girl on innocent summer evenings; but it was the *peke* that no one quite understood. Some said it was because of the sharp angle of the wood, while others talked of the mysterious carved stone that in the time of Queen Bess the villagers called the 'pieked stane'. 'T'was to do with them nuns and their goin' ons, like', they told darkly. She had heard this story a hundred times, and a hundred times she had searched for the carved stone on her journey to and from Savernake Park, but without success.

Pickrudge had been a wood since time immemorial but in Lettice's time the land was under cultivation for a while. Plough-teams went up there less and less often, however, and scrub, left unchecked, quickly developed into young woodland again. By the turn of the century, the cultivation strips no longer visible on the ground, even Lettice found it difficult to remember that Pickrudge had ever been anything but a Wood. She felt a little bit guilty about this for, as everyone in the country knows, it is always better never to let Nature take her course; but she and her neighbours stopped farming their Pickrudge holding simply because it was not worth the effort. It took each one of them a whole day several days a year, trekking with a slow-moving, cumbersome ox-team and tackle through the common fields over Windmill Hill and then across Boreham Down, simply to farm one single strip each. In addition, it was easier to let the scrub take over than go to the bother of planting up the land with oak for long-term timber and hazel for coppice-wood. Anyway, that was the lord's job, or that pushy Mr Pumphrey's. And the manorial tenants did not need more wood for their fires at home because they already had enough from Allen's Wood and elsewhere in Chichangles, and they all had their rights to keep taking it from there. Nor had they any reason to think other than that which had apparently always been would always be so.

The even tenor of subservient but not altogether unpleasant village life was, however, beginning to change rapidly as the century turned. Lettice, now in her seventies, was directly affected. Edward Pumphrey, a man of ever-increasing wealth and local power, was successfully pursuing his fairly ruthless policy of land acquisition, freehold and leasehold. He bought land outright, mainly off the manor. He bought up existing leases, particularly those of tenants with small plots who found to their innocent surprise that their right to labour over a bit of land actually had a cash value. And, as in Lettice's case, he made 'unrepeatable' offers for plots which he then consolidated into his own holdings. His moment came with Enclosure and the rent rise of 1802. This financially crippled many of the old tenants and those who, though relatively well-off like Lettice, simply did not have the cash income to cope with the new demands.

Lettice herself struggled on for three more years, first turning her flower-bed over to vegetables, not to eat but to sell for cash; but to little avail. She then had to sell her cows, for she now had nowhere to feed them, and next her pigs, for her single household did not generate enough waste to feed them on. Even her hens became scrawny and, scratching further afield for their scraps, took to laying away. And for the first time in her life, she knew real fear as, searching by herself for eggs along the new-laid hedges or picking wild fruits on the edge of the woods, more than once she was accosted in strange accents by rough-looking strangers, sometimes alone, sometimes in gangs, demanding coins and food and wanting to know where there was work and how far it still was to walk to Bath or Bristol. The village which had changed supposedly for the better was now a less happy place; perhaps the outside world was too. Or so Lettice wondered as she grew old in relative poverty, with most of her life-long friends now dead and younger acquaintances gone to the towns to look for work or to fight in what seemed ike never-ending wars.

It was as Nelson prepared for Trafalgar, then, that Lettice, her eyesight failing, peered through her cobwebby window and wondered why the day was overcast. The downs beyond had disappeared and, perhaps fortunately, she could hardly see the manor house and orchard now enjoyed by the pushy Edward Pumphrey.

'We live in an exciting new age of progress, Ma'am', he had declared to her grandiosely, some years ago now as he handed her a few sovereigns for her life-time's holding. 'Ours is a time of prosperity for all, when your land, my land, shall multiply the fruits of the earth an hundredfold.'

'If you say so, Mr Pumphrey', she had replied, politely but woodenly, avoiding his eye while inside she silently asked with some bitterness, 'Your land maybe, but where now is the land of Lettice Sweetapple?'

Lettice now smiled a little sadly to herself at the thought of what had come to pass; but she recognised that she was in any case too frail to work the land. She would have had to give it up sooner rather than later. Yet, she reflected, while land-holders will always change, in a very real sense the land, her land, would always be in place. She found that a comforting thought as she lay down to rest. She recalled that it was good land, which had given her a good living. She hoped that hers had also been a good life with it, and that others judged it to have been so.

Her remembrance of things past drifted as she drowsed. Then, with a sudden, startling clarity, she remembered days a long time ago, happy days when, as young girls, she and Jane Cook climbed in the manor orchard among the ripened fruit of regimented apple-trees. An old woman looked at them from the thatched stone cottage across the road, but they knew she could not see them. 'Sweet apples', Lettice would cry out to Jane, 'I'm a Sweetapple.' And Jane would laugh and somehow the name seemed so right.

Postscript

Although it is the landscape in which Lettice Sweetapple lived which is the subject of our study, rather than our eponymous 'heroine' herself, we nevertheless seize the opportunity of a reprint of the paperback published in 2000 to add to what we then knew about her. This information largely results from research by Alison Maddock of Bratton, Wiltshire. Lettice died much earlier than we had appreciated when we first wrote in 1998 so we added a Note to the Preface and mildly titivated the text to take this into account in 2000. Now we also know she was born rather earlier than we had imagined and was 77 when she died. Our Epilogue is therefore slightly out of kilter but, apart from two adjustments in it about her house and her age, we have left the text of 2000 alone.

Lettice was born in 1728 to John and Mary Sweetapple of Charlton, Andover, into a family well-established in north Hampshire and north Wiltshire. Her father's will of 1772 describes him as ' ... of Great Somerford gent', so she was born into a family at least of pretension. She was baptised at Minety, Wiltshire, and spent at least some of her childhood at Great Somerford, Wiltshire. Both her parents, however, were buried at Overton, suggesting the family was perhaps living there in the 1770s. John Sweetapple's widow, Lettice's mother, lived in Overton with her 50-year-old daughter probably from 1778, joined by the younger, unmarried brother Thomas, who outlived Lettice by fourteen years and who was born and died there. Lettice herself was afforded her funeral service in St. Michael's and All Saints, Overton, then in the form illustrated in our **colour plate 1**; yet curiously if understandably was buried, not at Overton but, 17 miles (25 km) distant, at Great Somerford on the same day, 5 August 1805. On Friday, 5 August 2005, at the start of a bi-centennial weekend during which about 100 people joined us in exploring 'the land of Lettice Sweetapple', we commemorated her life and funeral in the same church (now rebuilt as in **fig 50**).

Meanwhile, in the early years of the twenty-first century archaeological and historical research has continued on the downland, along the valley and in the woods of the land of Lettice Sweetapple to a degree which could enrich the content of this book without significantly changing the general tenor of its story. Such work now very much marches with an overt and public conservation agenda at local, regional, national and international levels. In 2008, the whole of Fyfield Down (**colour plates 8, 10, 14**), where in 1959 we began our explorations which eventually gave rise to the concept of 'the land of Lettice Sweetapple', was inscribed on the World Heritage List as part of the Stonehenge, Avebury and Associated Sites World Heritage Site.

Peter Fowler and Ian Blackwell
2009

Further Reading

Aston M. 1985 *Interpreting the Landscape* Batsford, London

Aston M. and Lewis C. (eds) 1994 *The Medieval Landscape of Wessex* Oxbow Monograph 46, Oxford

Bell M., Fowler P.J. and Hillson S.W. (eds) 1996 *The Experimental Earthwork Project 1960-92*, Council for British Archaeology Rsch. Rpt. 100, York

Beresford M. and Hurst J.G. (eds) 1989 (2nd ed.) *Deserted Medieval Villages* Alan Sutton, Gloucester

Fleming A. 1988 *The Dartmoor Reaves* Batsford, London

Fowler P. and Sharp M. *Images of Prehistory* 1990, Cambridge University Press (esp. the Avebury area, pp. 173-93)

Gelling M. 1993 (paperback) *Place-Names in the Landscape* Dent, London

Gingell C. 1992 *The Marlborough Downs: a later Bronze Age landscape and its origins* Wiltshire Archaeological and Natural History Society Monograph no. 1, Devizes

Gover J.E.B., Mawer A., and Stenton F.M. 1939 *The Place-Names of Wiltshire* (English Place-Name Society, vol. XVI) Cambridge University Press

Hoare R.C. 1821 The *Ancient History of North Wiltshire* London

Hodges R. 1991 *Wall-to-Wall History* Duckworth, London

Hostetter E. and Howe T.N. (eds.) 1997 *The Romano-British Villa at Castle Copse, Great Bedwyn* Indiana University Press, Bloomington

Jones M. 1986 *England before Domesday* Batsford, London

Malone C. 1989 *Avebury* Batsford/English Heritage, London

Morris R. 1989 *Churches in the Landscape* Dent, London

Pevsner N. 1963 *The Buildings of England: Wiltshire* Penguin, Harmondsworth

Powell B., Allen M. and Barnes I. 1996 *Archaeology in the Avebury Area, Wiltshire* Wessex Archaeology Rpt. 8, Salisbury

Rackham O.1990 (rev. ed., paperback) *Trees and Woodland in the British Landscape* Dent, London

Roberts B.K. 1996 *Landscapes of Settlement* Routledge, London

Smith A. C. 1885 *Guide to the British and Roman Antiquities of the North Wiltshire Downs in a Hundred Square Miles round Abury* Second edition, Wiltshire Archaeological and Natural History Society, Devizes

Taylor C. 1983 *Village and Farmstead* George Philip, London

VCH = Victoria County *History of Wiltshire*, esp. vols. 1, 2

Watts K. 1993 *The Marlborough Downs* Ex Libris Press, Bradford on Avon

Glossary

The following words etc. are used in the following sense in this book.
Warning: they may be used in a different sense elsewhere.

AD   anno domini, from the year of Our Lord i.e. AD 1 and after. NB: there was no such year as '0', AD or BC

Assart   to clear, or a clearing of, land for human use, characteristically woodland or stoney ground

BC   before Christ, 1 BC and earlier

Barrow   burial mound; *long*: much longer than wide in plan, in this area often with stone structures at the eastern, higher end, and parallel or slightly curved side ditches; of the fourth millennium BC for collective burial, though often re-used for burial and other purposes; *round*: circular in plan, usually with a ditch and a long and complex structural history; essentially for an original, single burial, characteristically 2200-1500 BC, and often re-used, not only for burials but as boundary markers etc.

Beaker   a particular type of pottery characteristic of *c*.2000 BC (**colour plate 31**), arguably but now unfashionably denoting a distinct, invasive people

Crop-mark   a difference in the growth of a crop occasioned by a buried archaeological feature, characteristically photographed from the air as a colour difference in cereals.

Demesne   land farmed directly by the lord

Earthworks   banks and ditches and other unevenesses in the surface of the ground caused by human construction and occupation, characteristically followed by desertion e.g. of a village

Knap   to strike flint on flint skilfully, to produce flint tools and, incidentally, many waste flakes

Lynchet   accumulation of plough-soil along a field edge, characteristically accentuated as a scarp on a slope by downhill drift, also as a result of cultivation, of soil in the field below. Not specific to any one period

Megalith(ic)   (made of) big stone(s)

Parch-mark   a particular type of crop-mark, occasioned by soil moisture deficiency in long dry periods causing a crop to ripen or 'burn off' differentially

Sarsens   blocks of a type of sandstone, characteristic of the study area

Time-periods
(all approx)

Palaeolithic	to 7000 BC	*Mesolithic*	7000-4000 BC
Neolithic	4000-2000 BC	*Bronze Age*	2000-700 BC
Early Iron Age	700-100 BC	*Late Iron Age*	100 BC-AD 43
Later prehistoric	2000 BC-AD 43	*Roman*	AD43-500
Early medieval	AD 500-1000	*Medieval*	1000-1600
Post-medieval	1600-1820		

Acknowledgements

In this book, as in the archive and the monograph, we draw on the skills, application and time of hundreds of people over 39 years, 1959-98. Many are acknowledged in the monograph, but here we can only offer our gratitude to them collectively and anonymously. Most were volunteers, although we could not also have done without the professional help of institutions such as the Wiltshire County Record Office and of the staff of the Wiltshire Archaeological and Natural History Society. Not once has an owner or tenant among those who own the land of Fyfield and the Overtons denied us access; and, perhaps in part because we were not always able to ask permission personally, we would especially thank them for allowing us to study on distant down and in unseen wood. We would also thank those many villagers who did not raise the alarm as we critically appraised the outside of their properties and they, from behind their twitching curtains, appraised our obviously suspicious behaviour.

This book has been written during the course of two other research projects, funded respectively by English Heritage and the Leverhulme Trust. Neither has directly supported work on the book itself, yet both have incidentally but significantly contributed to much of the academic study underlying these pages. Specific to this publication have been infrastructural support of the Department of Agricultural and Environmental Science, University of Newcastle upon Tyne, the graphic assistance of Kristian Strutt, and the photographic skills of Trevor Ermel, Monochrome, Newcastle upon Tyne. Most of the photographs are by one of the authors (PJF); the other provided 45; provided by others, and hereby gratefully acknowledged, are 23 and 36, reproduced by permission of the Committee for Air Photography, Cambridge University; colour plate 7, reproduced by permission of the Experimental Earthworks Committee; 4, 16 and 43 by N.U.Grudgings; 26 and 46 by Inigo Jones, former warden of the Fyfield Down National Nature Reserve; colour plate 25 by the Air Photographic Unit, Royal Commission on the Historical Monuments of England; and 32 and 68 by Gillian Swanton. We thank Elizabeth Fowler for her meticulous index.

Our greatest debt, indicated in our dedication, is to a farming family which, in so positively encouraging and supporting not only our project but many others too, has in effect, judging from the resultant publications alone, run a land-based scientific research institute throughout the second half of the twentieth century.

Index

NOTE

The modern parishes of West Overton and Fyfield absorbed the historic tithings and manors of West Overton, East Overton, Lockeridge, Shaw, Fyfield and part of Clatford. This index therefore unavoidably uses the same place names for different land units. To locate places it is necessary to refer to the maps on pages 14, 26, 74, 95, 98, 107, 142 and 147. All place names are in the modern county of Wiltshire except where otherwise stated. Word-by-word alphabetisation is not followed in entries, eg coins, houses, pottery and settlements where chronological entries are more logical. The black and white illustrations are indexed in **bold** type in their page sequence. The **colour plates** are indexed under **col pl** plus **number** at the end of the relevant index entry.

Other titles published by The History Press

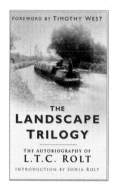

The Landscape Trilogy

LTC ROLT

L.T.C. Rolt was a pioneer of canal and railway preservation. Imbued with his love of England, these autobiographies, with a foreword by Timothy West and an introduction by Rolt's widow, Sonia, reveal landscapes populated by people, and by the machines which fascinated Rolt.

978 07509 4139 6   £12.99

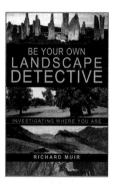

Be Your Own Landscape Detective

RICHARD MUIR

Reconstruction of the past is not a difficult task, and with Richard Muir as the expert guide the reader is soon brought face to face with a dazzling array of historical clues quite literally under his feet. Both accessible and informative, this guide from the leading popular writer on the history of the landscape demonstrates that the scenery of countryside and suburb can be read like a book.

978 07509 4333 8   £20.00

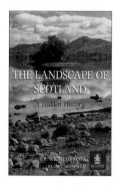

The Landscape of Scotland

C.R WICKHAM JONES

From lochs, coastlines and waterways, to highlands, forests and fields, this book examines how the lie of the Scottish land holds countless archaeological sites both above and below ground: farmsteads, castles, standing stones and many more. The sites are explained in terms of how and why they sprung up, for human, geological and climactic reasons. The book describes how the wealth of the land was extracted and exploited through mining and industry; how communities interacted with each other through trade and warfare; and how religion and burial were performed.

978 07524 1484 3   £16.99

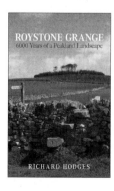

Roystone Grange

RICHARD HODGES

Describes the archaeology and history of a picturesque White Peak farm at Roystone Grange. Based upon fieldwork, this book dissects the sequence of prehistoric, Roman, medieval and modern farms, and also the fossilized fields and field walls. Illustrated with maps, plans, and photographs, it presents an impressive example of English landscape archaeology.

978 07524 3653 1   £17.99

If you are interested in purchasing other books published by The History Press, or in case you have difficulty finding any History Press books in your local bookshop, you can also place orders directly through our website

www.thehistorypress.co.uk